Nursery Management

Nursery Management

John Mason

Kangaroo Press

Acknowledgments

Contributors

Brian Collins, 'Bar Coding in the Nursery', Chapter 8
David Mason, 'Computers in the Nursery', Chapter 8

Staff at Australian Correspondence School:
Paul Plant B.App.Sc. (Hort.Tech.)
Iain Harrison Dip. Hort.Sc. MAIH, MRAIPR
Vicki Bailey B.App.Sc. (Hort.Tech.)

The author thanks the Horticultural Research & Development Corporation, the research arm of the Australian horticultural industries, for permission to reproduce information from the National Consumer and Retailer Study of Nursery Opportunities, 1991. He also thanks Elizabeth Cooling for her advice on nursery spray programs.

Drawings
Stephen Mason
Vicki Bailey
John Mason

Photographs
Leonie and John Mason

Front cover photos

Top left: In-ground production of tulips. Tulips covered by a tunnel greenhouse in winter promotes early flowering and helps the plants to develop stronger growth. The plastic cover is removed in spring. The harvested flowers can be sold on the cut flower market, and the bulbs divided for sale to nurseries. (Tesselar's Tulip Farm, Silvan, Victoria)

Top right: A well organised and decorative display such as this *Kalanchoe* collection can help to highlight and draw attention to plant lines which might otherwise go unnoticed.

Bottom left: Colour coding plants using pots assists quick identification of varieties. The *Coleus* are in red pots, other varieties are in different coloured pots.

Bottom right: Reinforced plastic sheeting draped over propagation beds provides protection on cold nights, or increases humidity as required.

Reprinted in 1996
First published in 1994 by Kangaroo Press Pty Ltd
3 Whitehall Road Kenthurst NSW 2156 Australia
P.O. Box 6125 Dural Delivery Centre NSW 2158
Printed in Hong Kong through Colorcraft Ltd

ISBN 0 86417 603 1

Contents

Metric Conversion Table

Area
Metric

1 square centimetre	= 0.155 square inch
	= 100 sq millimetres
1 square metre	= 1.196 square yards
	= 10,000 square centimetres
1 square kilometre	= 1,000,000 square metres
1 hectare	= 2.471 acres
	= 10,000 square metres

Imperial

1 square inch	= 6.452 square centimetres
	= 1/144 square foot
1 square foot	= 929 square centimetres
	= 0.0929 square metre
1 square yard	= 0.8361 square metres
	= 9 square feet
1 acre	= 0.4047 hectare
	= 4,860 square yards
	= 4,046.87 square metres

Length
Metric

1 millimetre	= 0.001 metre
1 centimetre	= 10 millimetre
	= 0.3937 inch
	= 0.01 metre
1 metre	= 3.281 feet
	= 1,000 millimetres
	= 100 centimetres

Imperial

1 inch	= 25.4 millimetres
	= 2.54 centimetres
1 foot	= 30.48 centimetres
	= 0.3048 metre
	= 12 inches
1 yard	= 0.9144 metre
	= 3 feet

1 Scope and Nature of the Nursery Industry

The nursery industry is literally a growing industry. It produces billions of plants every year, making major contributions to the forestry, vegetable, fruit, landscape, cut flower and parks industries. There will always be a demand for plants and in turn there will always be a need for nurseries.

Throughout the world, nurseries come in all types and sizes. Many are small family businesses, sometimes just a small hobby business to supplement the family's normal source of income. At the other end of the scale are large commercial businesses which employ dozens of people and grow millions of plants. However, all nurseries, large and small, need good management if they are to be financially viable. This book aims to show you ways to make a difference to the financial viability, hence the success, of any nursery, irrespective of size or type.

The Industry

The nursery industry has continued to be a growth industry in Australia and throughout much of the world for several decades, even through periods of recession. According to the Australian Bureau of Statistics the value of sales in the nursery industry in the 1989-90 financial year was $375 million ($270 million for nursery plant materials, $68 million for cut flowers and $37 million for cultivated turf). Within the category of nursery plant materials, sales of exotic trees and shrubs were valued at $51 million, Australian native trees and shrubs $36 million, ferns and indoor plants $33 million, and seedlings $32 million.

There is opportunity for new nurseries to establish, provided they are selective in what they grow and that they maintain adequate standards in the quality of plants they produce. There are increasing opportunities for nurseries to export plants, particularly to Asia and the Middle East.

It is important for nursery managers to be well informed about industry trends, demands and conditions. Nurseries sell living things, and like all living things, plants are subject to the influences of weather, and plagues of diseases and pests. Plants are also subject to changing fashions. A promotion on TV or in popular magazines can significantly change the way the public spends, even if it might only be a temporary change. Over a period of years, the demand for different types of plants may remain stable, but over shorter periods there can be very significant changes in the demand for one type of plant or another. It is essential to stay in tune with the market place and wherever possible foresee changes in demand before they occur. You should maintain contact with the magazines, professional associations and gardening experts who can tell you about what is to be promoted next, or what plants will be in oversupply or undersupply in the near future.

Types of nurseries

In the past, nurseries were involved in almost all aspects of the production and culture of plants. They grew a wide variety of plants, and they sold them both wholesale and retail, as well as supplying a wide range of allied products and services. Today all but the largest nurseries tend to specialise.

Nurseries can be classified in many different ways; for example:

• according to what they grow, such as natives, exotics, seedlings, cottage garden plants, bonsai or bulbs;
• how they grow it, such as in-ground production or in containers;
• even the size of plants they produce, such as tubestock, small pots/containers, or advanced stock.

Nurseries which try to do everything rarely succeed. New nurseries should consider the following options carefully and define the scope of their operation to fit their resources, skills and knowledge.

Produce, Grow On or Sell?

There are three main types of nurseries: production, growing-on and retail. Production nurseries propagate plants and wholesale them to growing-on nurseries, or sell directly to retail nurseries, landscapers, parks departments, etc. Growing-on nurseries buy small plants which are potted into larger size containers or planted out and grown on to a larger size, adding value to their original purchase. Retail nurseries buy plants from production nurseries, then resell them at a profit. In many cases nurseries will be a combination of two, sometimes all three, types.

What to Grow?

It has often been said that the downfall of a nursery manager is 'He/she is too much of a plant collector and not enough of a businessperson'. Most people who work with plants love plants, and it is very easy to be tempted to grow the types of plants you love most. This is often the nurseryperson's 'Achilles heel'! It is essential to choose what you grow carefully. It is pointless growing lots of plants if there is no demand for them.

Some plant varieties require more space than others. Sprawling climbers or ground covers can take up a lot of room, tall slender trees will take less. Slow-growing plants don't have to be sold as soon as they are good enough for sale, but fast-growing plants deteriorate fast so must be sold quickly, unless you have the resources to continually keep potting them up into larger containers.

Some of the main choices are:

Trees and shrubs — both natives and exotics
Seedlings — mostly vegetables and annual flowers
Indoor or tropical plants
Grafted trees — fruit and ornamental

Ferns	Bulbs
Conifers	Water plants
Herbs	Bonsai
Perennials	Roses

You may choose to be a general nurseryperson growing or selling a wide range of plant types; to choose a theme, such as bonsai or cottage gardens; or to concentrate on a specific type or variety of plant, such as carnations, fuchsias or roses.

In-ground production of iris. Iris flowers grown in broad-acre rows can be harvested and sold as a cut flower, before dividing the rhizomes for sale each year. An appropriate amount of plant material must be kept to maintain stock for the following season's production of flowers and rhizomes.

Chrysanthemum cuttings placed directly into a bed of perlite. When the roots form, the plants can be removed and sold as bare-rooted cuttings or potted direct into the open ground.

How to Grow?

Plants can be grown in the ground or in containers. Plants grown in the ground are dug up immediately before sale, or transplanted and grown on in containers. Plants grown in containers may be sold in the same containers or may be potted up prior to sale.

Container growing uses mainly imported soil mixes (growing media). In-ground growing can take more space, might require a little more labour in some respects than container growing, and requires the nursery to be sited on suitable soil.

Comparison of container versus in-ground nursery production

Container	*In-ground*
Plants can be transported and sold in their containers, with little disturbance to the plant.	Plants must be lifted from the ground and packaged in a way that minimises damage to the plant.
Containers can be readily moved if necessary during production.	In-ground stock difficult to move during production.
Soil/growing media must be brought into the nursery to grow plants in.	Plants generally lifted and sold bare-rooted—soil is left behind and can be reused/cultivated.
Soils/growing media readily sterilised in small batches to reduce pest and disease problems.	Harder to control pest and disease problems.
Container-grown rootstocks harder to quickly bud or graft.	Easier to bud/graft rootstocks in-ground as the rootstock will not move too much as you do the graft—due to roots securing the plant.
Root ball restricted by size and shape of container.	Plants grown in-ground have greater opportunities for root zone development.
Restricted/limited amounts of growing media for plants' roots makes careful watering critical.	Watering less critical due to greater opportunities for root zone development and lower water from soil.

Nursery Standards

A nursery must set and adhere to certain standards if it is going to operate profitably. These standards can be broken down into three main groups:

1. Cost efficiency standards
2. Quality standards
3. Size standards

Cost Efficiency

There must be a sound relationship between the cost of production and the sales price. Both of these monetary figures must be constantly monitored and maintained at an acceptable level to ensure any business remains profitable. It is important to remember that a good nursery manager must not only be capable of producing and/or maintaining good quality plants and allied products, he or she must also be able to sell them profitably.

Cost of Production + Profit = Sales Price

In order to control your cost effectiveness, you must understand (and control) all factors which influence the cost of production. You may also need to make adjustments to your sales price figure in order to maintain an acceptable profit figure.

Cost of production is influenced by the following:
• Cost of site — lease/rent value or purchase costs.
• Cost of site services — power, gas, water, etc.
• Cost of materials — soil, pots, fertilisers, etc.
• Cost of unsold plants — a certain proportion of stock may be lost, may die, or may just become unsaleable. Some nurseries budget as much as 30% of stock being thrown away.
• Labour costs — this should include your own time as well as your employees', and don't forget holiday pay, superannuation requirements, health cover, etc.
• Advertising/promotion — printing, advertising in magazines, etc.
• Selling costs — transportation, invoicing, etc.
• Taxation (don't forget payroll tax, income tax, etc).

Profit
This figure should be over and above money which you earn as wages. If you are only working for wages (with no profit), then you would be better putting your money into a different form of investment and going to work for someone else.

Profit should be greater than the interest rate which you could get by investing your money elsewhere. Profit should normally be at least 15-20%. If the nursery is only small, then the profit margin should be larger. If the nursery is large, then the profit per plant can be kept lower. Profit in this situation comes through *quantity* of sales.

Sales Price
The figure which a plant is sold for can vary considerably. Retail price is normally about twice the wholesale price. This being the case, the wholesaler depends upon selling in large numbers in order to maintain profitability. Wholesale price varies considerably. Generally speaking, this figure is affected by two things:

1. The nurseryperson's reliability of supply.
If the wholesaler is well established and known to be a reliable source of plants, they can demand a higher price.

2. Quality of plants offered.
Higher prices are only paid for top quality stock.

Quality Standards

The following factors are of concern when considering the quality of plants:
• General health
Does the plant show evidence of pest or disease damage, dead leaves, burned leaves, markings on stems, or lack of vigour?
• Hardness or softness of tissue
Has the plant been hardened off, or will it be susceptible to fertiliser burn, frost, wind, sun, etc?
• Uniformity
Plants of a particular variety should be grown and sold in the same sized pot, the same colour pot, and have the same type of label. They should all be the same shape and size (roughly).
• Labels
Picture labels are preferred to printed labels without a picture. Tie-on labels may be preferred to stick-in (soil) labels because they cannot be removed easily and put with a different plant. Stick-in labels are, however, generally quicker to place in position than tie-on labels. Hand written labels do not generally provide as much information as commercially printed ones, and the writing often fades or runs, making them hard to read.

Size Standards

In the USA, the American Association of Nurserymen has set standards for nursery stock which are generally followed throughout that country. The system in Australia is not so formal. There are however unwritten standards which are generally adhered to. Plants which are presented in the wrong type of container are usually more difficult to sell.

Examples
Generally containerised plants are grown in plastic pots. Tins are rarely accepted today. Plastic bags are sometimes used, but are not nearly as widely accepted as rigid plastic pots.

Certain types of plants are generally sold in certain sized pots. Most trees and shrubs for the home garden are sold in 6 inch (125 mm) or 8 inch

(200 mm) pots. Herbs and indoor plants are usually sold in smaller plastic pots (e.g. 75 or 100 mm). Seedling vegetables and flowers are sold in plastic punnets. Advanced plants are sold in 2 gallon (10 litre) plastic buckets. Seedling grown plants for use as farm trees or for large-scale revegetation are often sold in 2 inch (50 mm) tubes. Deciduous trees and roses are sold bare-rooted over winter.

Starting Out

New nurseries, like many other small businesses, often fail because they haven't been properly planned. Nurseries can be started with minimal cash investment, but the size of the operation must be geared to the amount of cash invested. If the initial investment is small, then the nursery should be small and grow slowly. Even if a sizeable investment is made initially, it is wise to retain up to one-third of the cash available to carry the business for the first couple of years. Nursery profits can fluctuate greatly from year to year. If the first year is a bad season because of pests, diseases, bad weather or poor sales, then a reserve of cash is necessary to carry the nursery through to the second year.

A new nursery manager is usually limited by a lack of skills, poor knowledge of the market, and small reserves of money available to develop the operation. It is possible to start a profitable part-time nursery in the backyard. This type of operation will supplement a normal income, and at the same time allow you to learn from your experiences. A serious business venture is quite different though — you don't have the time to learn by making mistakes!

New nurserypersons should avoid growing the more difficult plants. These plants generally require more time and sophisticated equipment to grow them. This means that they are more expensive to deal with. Plants which require a greater length of time to bring to a saleable size should also be avoided until the nursery is generating enough sales to keep the nursery profitable while the plants are growing.

New nurserypersons are advised to produce plants in the standard packaging (e.g. 125 mm plastic pots). You know that the product will usually be saleable in this packaging!

Low shrubs and ground covers are generally in higher demand in urban areas than large shrubs and trees. The highest demand for large shrubs and trees is in the rural community. A plant with a flower on it is almost always more saleable.

Revamping An Established Nursery

There is always room for improvement, even in the best run nursery. A good nursery manager will keep an open mind, and will continually review the way things are done in the nursery industry, and look for better, more up-to-date and profitable ways of doing things.

Tasks such as the following should be happening continually:
• Looking for better prices for materials (e.g. pots, labels, stakes, potting media, etc).
• Reducing the numbers grown of some plants and increasing the numbers grown of others, in response to changes in consumer demand.
• Upgrading equipment.
• Staff training.
• Refining propagation methods for each plant variety that you grow.
• Analysing the success of marketing (e.g. compiling statistics on the response to promotions and the sales achieved from month to month).
• Calculating and analysing the profit and adjusting prices accordingly.

Organisation is the key

You can increase profitability by simply organising and planning what you do in a nursery. Planning should be an ongoing process, not something you start, then finish and forget about once a nursery has commenced operations. There are basic questions which should be asked over and over as you constantly review what your nursery is producing or selling, how you are producing or obtaining those products, and how you market your products.

The aim of good organisation and planning should be to:

• Reduce wasted time
Keep asking yourself, 'Can I get the same work done in less time if I do things differently?' In some cases

mechanisation of tasks may save considerable time and labour. In other cases simply rearranging the placement of propagating and potting-up benches will speed up the flow of plants and materials into and out of propagation areas.

• Reduce wasted facilities and equipment
Keep asking yourself, 'Can I do the same work just as well (or nearly as well) without the expense of that extra equipment?' You should only buy extra equipment because it will lead to extra profit. It's a trap to buy equipment because everyone else does, without giving serious consideration to how it will affect your profitability. It is sometimes more cost effective to hire some types of equipment, particularly equipment that, while necessary to the nursery's operation, is only used infrequently. When hiring equipment, however, make sure it is readily available when you will require it.

• Reduce wasted materials
Be self critical. It is easy for expenses to increase because potting mix gets spilt on the floor; because you buy too many labels and pots which can degrade or break down over time, or get damaged if stored incorrectly; or because you fertilise or spray more often than is necessary. You should predetermine what you need and buy that quantity, with perhaps a little extra in case of losses from accidents or sudden demand for products. It is a mistake to buy materials when you need them, without having calculated what your requirements should have been.

Remember money spent on excess materials, that are sitting there doing nothing except taking up valuable space, is a wasted asset that can be used elsewhere and more profitably in the nursery's operation.

• Make the most efficient use of labour
This is particularly important if you are employing staff, but also applies to getting the most from your own labour. It is important to plan ahead what tasks each worker will be undertaking the next day, week, or even further ahead. This way both staff and employers know what has to be done rather than continually wasting time trying to sort out what they are supposed to be doing. It is also important to have suitably trained staff and the right mix of staff. There is little point in having, for example, staff busily propagating plants if you don't have the support staff available to care for those plants once propagated, or to do the marketing and transporting.

2 The Nursery Site

The size, location and internal characteristics of a nursery site must be appropriate for the type of nursery you are operating.

Size

The amount of land required for a successful operation can vary from 0.1 hectare (1/4 acre) up to hundreds of hectares. The amount of land you acquire may depend on the following:
- Cost of land — you may have to compromise your ideals for what you can afford.
- What is available — you may be unable to get the exact size you want; e.g. if you need a 1 hectare (2.5 acre) lot, land might only be selling in 2 hectare (5 acre) lots in your preferred locality.
- Spacing of plants — will the plants be kept close together or spread out?

There are viable commercial nurseries operating out of backyards with as little as 300 to 400 square metres of space devoted to plants. Some of these backyard businesses generate enough income to support a family, but good management is particularly critical for such businesses where space is at a premium. Many of the largest nurseries have started out as small backyard operations.

Propagation nurseries and tissue culture operations generally require less space because the plants don't take up much room, and they don't need to be kept and grown on for long before they are sold. There are a large number of plants produced with respect to space used in these nurseries, and a high income per unit area.

Nurseries which deal with valuable collectors' plants (e.g. rare plants, bonsai, carnivorous plants and orchids) may also require less space than other nurseries because they are able to generate more money per plant.

General retail nurseries can vary in size from a small shop in a suburban shopping centre to a large regional garden centre that may be five or more hectares in size. Retail nurseries which have a fast turnover of plants need less space because they don't need room to hold or store plants for lengthy periods between sales.

Advanced plant nurseries generally require considerable space because plants may be grown for several years either in containers or in-ground before being sold. Nurseries that grow grafted plants or advanced trees in field rows will require at least one hectare of land to be a viable operation.

Planning Restrictions

Various government authorities have control over the way land can be used. Planning departments in both local and state governments can prevent a nursery from being operated in some locations and under some conditions. The worst nightmare for any business person can be to have a profitable business closed down or forced to restrict its operations because it doesn't have the right permits.

Before you start or buy a nursery, you should thoroughly check that the intended use is allowed in the location being considered. If buying, perhaps your purchase contract should state 'subject to appropriate planning permits'.

In reality, authorities often bend the rules or overlook nurseries which do not have appropriate permits, provided no-one complains. Once a complaint is lodged though, the authorities can be forced to act, and sometimes even long-established nurseries can be affected. There was a case in Victoria in the mid 1980s where more than thirty local nurseries were forced to close or restrict operations because one licensed nursery made a complaint.

Site Considerations

Before buying land or buying an existing nursery site you should check the following:
• Slope — sloping sites will require earthworks for buildings and terracing for areas to place plants. Earthworks can be very expensive!
• Drainage — speak with neighbours. Consider all parts of the property.
• Flooding — is the land prone to flooding?
• Bushfires — is it prone to fires?
• Access — can you get onto the site easily? Can you get around all parts of the site easily?
• Existing facilities and services — including buildings, water, power and phone.
• Microclimates — trees provide shade and some protection against frosts, but can restrict light and reduce growth rates. (This is an advantage with some plants, and a disadvantage with other plants).

Location

The location of a nursery is determined primarily by the following factors:
• Proximity to markets — marketing costs are reduced if customers or transportation to customers are in close proximity.

• Cost of land — this varies from place to place. The closer to city centres, the more expensive the land will be expected to become.
• Access to services — if you have to pay for water, power, phone, etc. to be brought some distance to your property, this can be expensive. The closer you are to these services, the cheaper the services will be.
• Soil type — some soils are cheaper to do earthworks on. Foundations to structures may become expensive if the soil is very sandy or has a large proportion of expandable clay. If you plan to grow plants in the soil (i.e. stock plants or in-ground production), then the better the soil fertility and quality the easier the plants will be to grow.
• Climate — consider rainfall, frost, hail, wind, etc. varies from locality to locality, even over the space of just a few kilometres. Speak to the weather bureau to obtain details.
• Aspect — sites facing north get more sun in Australia and can be utilised to bring plants into flower a little earlier than south-facing sites. Alternatively, southern slopes may be the best site for a nursery growing cooler climate plants.
• Isolation from diseases — this is an advantage if the nursery is growing plants which have particular disease or pest problems. Nursery hygeine is important to prevent disease entry into your nursery.
• Air quality — consideration should be given to nearby industrial businesses. Pollutants can contaminate the air and deposit residue on nursery stock. If there is a pungent smell in the air, prospective costumers may be persuaded away from your business. Chemical drifts from adjoining properties (e.g. farmers using aerial sprays) may also affect nursery plants.
• Water — availability and quality is very important. Chemicals in the water may result in toxic symptoms or slow death of stock plants. The conductivity of the water needs to be measured to indicate salt concentrates in the water. The higher the conductivity, the less suitable it is for plant culture.
• Labour supply — if you plan to set up your nursery away from a populated district you may have difficulty in hiring staff willing to travel or with adequate horticultural experience.
• Security — from both animal and human damage. Native and domestic animals can affect nursery production by eating stock plants, damaging irrigation systems, and knocking over and breaking plants. Humans may cause damage through

vandalism or theft. Security is essential, whether the nursery uses high fence systems or hired security personnel. A staff member living on site will also provide security.

• Government regulations — all regulations, compliances and statutory requirements must be considered. Each city or shire will have slightly different regulations with regard to building codes, hygiene practices, occupational health and safety, operation hours, signs, etc.

Designing Facilities in the Nursery

Administrative offices
These should be located in a central position to give control over production, sales, receiving and despatching of stock, etc.

Circulation and parking
Convenient access and parking is especially critical in retail nurseries. Carpark areas for the public should be well marked, with clear signposting and preferably covered with hard surfacing material such as asphalt. Avoid creating sharp bends in driveway areas.

Receiving and depatch areas will need sufficient room for large trucks to turn around. Elevated docks and assembly areas for stock should also be considered for ease of loading/unloading.

You will also need to consider provision of vehicular access within the nursery; for example, to storage areas, for shifting large quantities of plants, or for moving heavy advanced plants.

Employee facilities
Carparking facilities, lunchrooms, supervisors' offices, toilet blocks, etc. for nursery employees need to be considered at the planning stage. Clean, neat

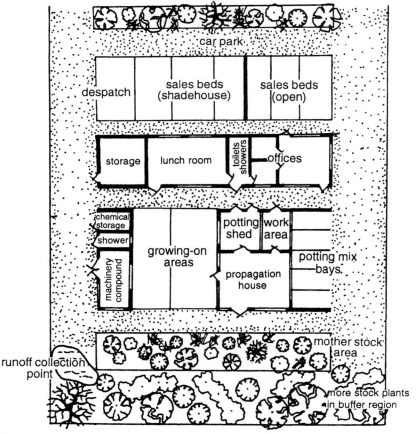

Layout of a wholesale nursery (general container plants)

facilities will help maintain employee morale. It is best to keep staff facilities separate from the public areas of the nursery.

Public areas
The appearance of public areas in the nursery is extremely important for attracting and maintaining customers. Facilities for the public include display gardens, playground areas for children, public toilets and sales areas. These should be designed so that they can be maintained at the highest standard at

all times, e.g. paths and walkways should be covered with cement or blue metal so they can easily be kept free of rubbish and weeds.

Landscaped areas are a useful way of advertising the nursery's plants so it is well worth expending some effort in this direction. The carpark and the sales areas are both excellent areas for including display beds which will attract the customers' attention.

Play areas for visitors' children should also be considered as this will not only provide your

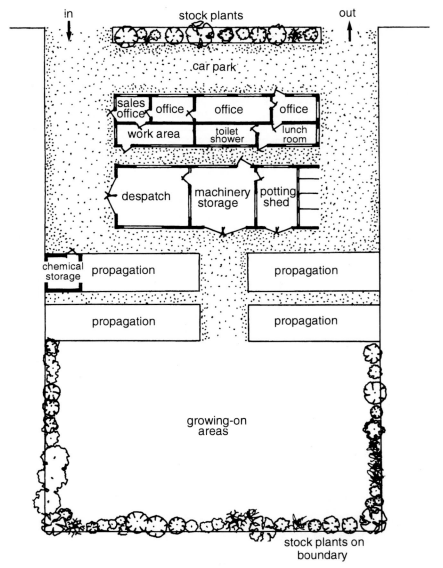

Layout of a wholesale nursery (propagation/tubestock nursery)

Lockup storage area. This provides secure storage of expensive items, as well as dangerous chemicals and tools.

customers with more browsing time, but also save plants from being damaged by bored children. It is best to site the playground in a position where the parents can still easily keep an eye on the kids.

Storage areas

Equipment, tools, potting mixes, fertilisers and pesticides need to be stored in secure lockable buildings or storage cabinets which are conveniently located to the production areas. Chemicals should be stored in a separate dry area.

Drainage network

Surface water, including rainwater and water from overhead sprinklers, should be immediately removed from exposed surfaces. If the nursery is a retail venture, the customers will not want to walk through water to get a plant. There is also the possibility that customers and employees will slip and injure themselves on wet surfaces.

Puddles of water also provide breeding grounds for diseases and many insects. A network of drainage channels will help prevent these problems.

Production areas

The following main areas can be included in production areas:

1. Mother stock area

Mother stock (also referred to as 'stock plants') are plants which are grown, usually in-ground, specifically for the purpose of providing a source of cuttings. Therefore it is essential that this area is positioned so that plants will be of the highest quality to give vigorous, disease-free cutting material (i.e. well-cultivated, fertile soils with provision of adequate watering).

In larger nurseries, this is usually a separate area; in smaller nurseries, plants in display gardens are used for this purpose.

2. Propagation area

This area contains greenhouses, usually with bottom heating, and hardening-off areas (depending on the climate and plants grown this may include polyhouses without additional heating, shadehouses and fairly protected areas in the open).

3. Potting up area

The potting up area needs to be located near the propagation area. The area should be under cover and will include provision for pots, soils, potting machines, benches and trolleys. It should also be conveniently located to storage areas to avoid having to shift potting media, pots, etc. around the nursery.

4. Growing-on area

After hardening off, plants are placed in blocks in the open until they are ready to sell.

3 Production Systems

There are many different ways of producing plants although most plants are produced commercially by either seed or cutting propagation. Tissue culture or 'micropropagation' techniques carried out in a laboratory are sometimes used where very large numbers of one plant variety are required quickly. Other plants are traditionally produced by budding and grafting onto seed or cutting-grown rootstocks (e.g. roses, deciduous fruit and ornamental trees). Division and separation are commonly used for the propagation of bulbs and herbaceous perennials.

Other propagation techniques (e.g. layering or marcotting) may be important in the propagation of some specific types of plants, however they are relatively insignificant when taking a broad view of the nursery industry.

There are normally four stages stage in nursery plant production:
1. Propagation
2. Transplanting
3. Growing on
4. Marketing the fully grown plant

Each of these stages usually requires specialised skills. Large nurseries have the luxury of being able to organise their staff to allow them to specialise in one or two of these stages of production, but smaller nurseries need to employ experienced staff, or train staff to be competent in all stages of production.

Propagation

A skilled propagator can propagate large numbers of plants very quickly and with minimum losses due to disease, rough handling or poor techniques. If a propagator can get cuttings to strike faster, seed to germinate quicker, or grafts to 'take' (i.e. grow together) sooner, then the plants are produced in less time, take up less space in the nursery, require less nurturing, and hence profitability can be increased significantly.

The quality and quantity of work achieved by a propagator can vary greatly from nursery to nursery. It is not uncommon for one good propagator to produce the same quantities of plants as three less experienced or less efficient propagators at another nursery.

Some nurseries choose to avoid this stage of production because of the degree of skill required and because it is an area of commercial vulnerability. They find it easier to purchase rooted cuttings, tubestock or tissue cultured plants and grow them on for resale.

Improving Production Efficiency

There are several factors which will affect the efficiency achieved in the production of seedlings or rooted cuttings. Some of the more obvious factors are listed below. You may be able to think of others.

Quality of work

General

Have the propagating equipment and containers/trays been cleaned/sterilised?
Has the propagating mix been mixed thoroughly and sterilised?
Have the seeds or cuttings been correctly labelled?

Cuttings

How well is the cutting prepared and planted?
Has the propagator damaged the cutting material excessively? (This would increase the likelihood of pest or disease damage.)
Has the correct amount of leaf been removed?
Has the cutting been placed in the propagating media properly?
Has the cutting been treated in a way which will minimise drying out throughout the cutting operation?

Seed

Has viable (fresh) seed been used?
Has the seed been adequately separated from fruits or pods?
Has the seed been sown evenly and at a suitable density? Seeds sown too heavily will be overcrowded and consequently of poorer quality. Seeds sown too thinly wastes valuable space and materials.
Has the seed been sown at a suitable depth? More seeds are lost from sowing too deeply than by sowing at a too shallow depth. Seeds sown deeply will also take longer to emerge after germination.

Selection of the most appropriate technique

General

What time of the year is the operation carried out?
What type of propagating medium is used, e.g. sand/peat, sand, vermiculite, growool, open ground, perlite bed, gravel bed, nutrient agar?

Cuttings

What type of cutting is used, e.g. semi-hardwood, hardwood, softwood, tip cuttings, older wood, leaf bud, leaf, root; 4 cm long, 6 cm long, etc?

What additional treatments have been carried out on the cuttings, e.g. hormones, disinfecting drenches?

Seed

Has a suitable pre-germination treatment been used, e.g. scarification, stratification, hot water?

Aftercare

Where are the seed trays or cuttings placed after planting?
Are they exposed to the elements, or placed in a glasshouse, cold frame or hot bed, etc?
How frequently are they watered?
Are they watered by hand, manual sprinklers or automatic sprinklers?

Growth stimulation

Have any techniques been used to stimulate germination or root growth, e.g. bottom heat, wounding, intermittent misting, fogging?

Cost of materials

Are the seed or cuttings placed in a pot, in a bed or in the ground?
How many seeds or cuttings can be fitted into a particular space? More cuttings or seeds per unit space is more cost efficient as long as they are not overcrowded.
What materials costs are incurred? This includes the cost of pots, propagating mix, labels, hormones, greenhouses, hotbeds, etc.

Labour costs

Do you have ready access to propagation material? Consider the time involved obtaining seeds or cuttings.
How many seeds can you sow, or cuttings can you prepare and plant per hour?
What time is involved in aftercare, i.e. watering, weeding, spraying, fertilising, etc?

Cuttings of *Lavandula dentata* placed directly into tubes. For cuttings which form roots easily, this procedure saves the task of transplanting the rooted cuttings from trays or beds into tubes.

Are the propagation greenhouses close to the propagating area? Does it take time to transfer cuttings or seed trays from one area to another? Will the variety of plant grown require more attention than other plants?

Success rate

What proportion of seeds germinate, or cuttings planted actually form roots?

How long does it take for the seeds to germinate or for cuttings to form roots? This must be related back to the cost of the space, i.e. if the cuttings or seed take up a lot of space in a hotbed, consider that the hotbed costs money to buy and run. The seed which germinates more quickly or cuttings which strike faster are generally less expensive to produce.

Are you propagating varieties which have a high success rate?

All of these factors (and others) will have a bearing on the cost of producing a plant from seed or by cutting. Some of these factors will be more significant than others. Some may account for 10, 20 or 30% of the cost; others might only account for a very small proportion of the cost.

Practical Exercise

Prepare a pot of cuttings or tray of seeds and estimate the cost of production for each plant produced:

1. Write down step by step what is to be done:
    a) Obtain propagating material.
    b) Assemble materials, e.g. containers, media, labels.
    c) Prepare and plant cuttings or sow seed.
    d) Water and place in greenhouse.
    e) Aftercare for 'x' months, including watering, fertilising, pest and disease control, etc.
2. List the materials/equipment required and estimate their costs.
3. Prepare several pots of cuttings, or trays of seeds. Time yourself. Note how many cuttings have been placed in each pot, or seeds sown in each tray/container.

4. Estimate the aftercare time expected and the proportion of cuttings you expect to strike, or seeds to germinate.
5. Estimate the cost of producing one plant by cutting or from seed (using the material/equipment costs and labour requirements established in the previous steps). This will require you to set an hourly rate for your labour costs. Be realistic, and don't forget you have to include a labour cost component as well as all the extras such as compulsory super-annuation or health cover, payroll taxes, holiday pay, etc.

Transplanting

Transplanting is the taking of newly propagated plants from the propagating medium and placing them in a growing medium in a manner that minimises damage, or reduces any setback in growth of the plant. It is not always as straightforward as might be expected, particularly with tissue cultured plants. When a plant is taken from one environment to a different one, the plant may experience 'transplanting shock', which under extreme circumstances can cause the plant to die. You need to pay careful attention to where plants came from and ease them into their new environment. The nursery must have facilities to do this, e.g. greenhouses, shadehouses and heating.

Tissue cultured plants are the most difficult to transplant and establish in soil. Plants taken from a greenhouse, or propagated in a warm climate and moved into areas with cooler climates can also be difficult to establish and maintain.

Two critical factors at this stage are cleanliness (so you don't expose the plant unnecessarily to diseases or pests), and a good quality growing medium (because this will be with the plant until it is sold).

Transplanting seedlings

Ideally seedlings should be transplanted as soon as possible after they have emerged. This will vary to some degree according to the type of plant you are growing. Those with larger seedlings can generally be handled earlier than smaller ones. Normally seedlings will be transplanted once the first or second true leaves have appeared.

Trays or flats of seedlings can be removed to a protected propagation area. They should be well watered, and if possible allowed to drain for a short time, prior to lifting the seedlings. The seedlings can then be carefully lifted from their containers and gently pulled apart, taking great care to minimise damage to roots. Retain as much of the propagating medium as possible around the roots, and only remove small clumps or groups of seedlings at a time to prevent roots drying out excessively.

Seedlings which have been grown in-ground or in large beds can be carefully lifted and immediately transferred to a protected area for transplanting. The seedlings can be kept moist by temporarily storing them in a container of water, a plastic bag, or other moist material. If possible only lift small amounts of seedlings at a time to ensure they are not left lying around for any length of time.

The containers (e.g. flats, pots or punnets) that the seedlings are to be grown-on in should be filled with a suitable growing medium, and a planting hole or holes made with a dibble stick. The roots of the seedling are inserted into the hole and the growing medium is pressed gently around the roots to ensure good contact. For large flats or containers, dibble boards can be used to make large numbers of holes at the one time. The transplanted seedlings should be watered immediately, and as soon as possible placed in a protected growing-on environment.

Transplanting cuttings

Rooted cuttings can be transplanted in a similar manner to seedlings. Containers of cuttings are removed from propagation areas and the cuttings are carefully knocked out of the container. If root development is evident, then cuttings can be carefully pulled apart, retaining as much propagation medium as possible around the roots. Cuttings with sufficient root development can be transplanted into suitable containers, while cuttings with little or no root development can be placed back into the propagation medium, and returned to the propagation house or area. Cuttings with obvious decay of their base or stem should be discarded. All of the cuttings, including those which have not yet formed roots, should be watered thoroughly after transplanting.

Potting up plants

Plants are potted for the following reasons:

1. They are getting too large for the pot they are in and need more room to grow.
2. You want them to grow at a faster rate to produce a larger plant in less time.
3. You want the plant in a different container — something which looks better or is more functional.
4. You want to root prune the plant. This promotes the development of new healthy feeder roots. Root pruning may also be undertaken to remove diseased roots.
5. You want to put the plant into a better growing medium.

Removing the plant from the container:

• For small to medium containers, tip the container upside down and gently shake it; if this doesn't work tap the ridge of the pot on the edge of a wheelbarrow or bench.
• The root ball should be moist before removing it from the container.
• If the plant is pot bound, soak it (immerse) thoroughly in water first.
• Large pots may need to be cut away from the plant.

Potting machines

Potting machines were developed to reduce manual labour, increase efficiency and improve output. Potting machines may be simple, assisting with supplying potting mix to the pot, or complex, carrying out a large part of the overall potting operation. There are many different systems available. They can carry out or assist with any number or combination of the following tasks:

• Filling the pot with potting mix. This is usually achieved by dropping mix from a mechanically filled hopper above. Mix can be dropped manually or automatically, and if required, in predetermined quantities.
• Placing or holding a plant in position as the potting mix is filled around it. The plant might be extracted automatically from standard sized propagation containers such as plugs used for vegetable or flower seedlings, or fed by hand into the machine.
• Feeding pots one at a time into the machine. The

pots might be lined up onto a conveyor belt by hand, or mechanically taken from stacks one by one and fed onto a conveyor.

• Transferring potted plants away from the machine. Once potted, the plants might be placed manually or automatically onto a conveyor belt which takes them to a point from which they can be loaded onto barrows or trailers and carried to growing-on areas.

Potting machines are never a 100% automatic operation. They can have things go wrong, and they need a skilled operator to watch them, feed the raw materials in (i.e. plants, pots and potting mix), and take the potted plants away.

Potting machines can be one of the nursery's most important investments. They can be considerably expensive to purchase, but they can greatly decrease the nursery's wages bill. A good potting machine can halve the number of staff needed in a nursery. The cost of the machines will vary depending on the features desired in the machine. Before even looking at machines, it is essential to determine what functions it should perform.

Possible problems to consider:
• Potting machines working with abrasive soil components (e.g. sand) will suffer more wear and tear than some other types of machines.
• When a pot separating device is being used, get samples from your pot supplier and check that they work before buying the machine. The same pot size from different manufacturers doesn't always separate well.
• The potting medium needs to be of uniform quality to work in many types of machines.
• Is the potting speed appropriate for your needs?
• Some machines have limited accessibility, causing congestion, particularly if several people are working around the machine at the same time.
• Does the machine fit comfortably into your working area? Is your shed big enough and can staff move around the machine easily?

High speed rotary seeder. (Manufactured by ATG Williames P/L)

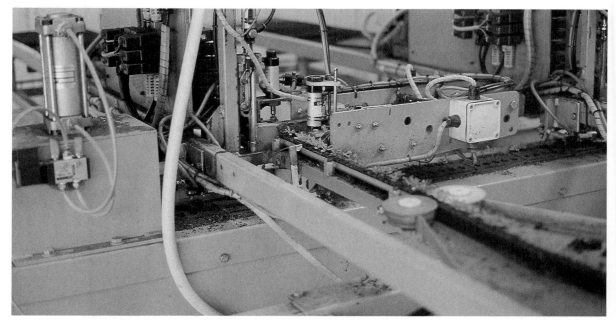

Selective automatic transplanting machine. (Manufactured by ATG Williames P/L)

Potting shrubs and trees

These can be potted at most times of the year, ideally when the plant is actively growing, but be aware there will be some transplant shock, and a recovery period will be required afterwards. Potting can cause flower bud drop, so if you want flowers do not pot close to the flowering period. If you pot in summer, the plant may suffer from water stress and will need to be closely watched for at least a few days.

• Don't pot up in windy or sunny places — drying of plant roots can occur very rapidly.
• Pot in a clean place (a clean shed or on a washed concrete base) to minimise disease problems.
• Don't pot on a very hot day.
• Put plants into a cool protected position for at least a few weeks after potting.

Potting bare-rooted plants

Most plants from in-ground nurseries are lifted for transplanting in a bare-rooted state. In particular, this includes many deciduous plants, such as grafted fruit trees, ornamental trees and roses. They are usually lifted when the plant is in a dormant state during mid to late winter because the plants will suffer minimal transplant shock during this period.

The plants are usually lifted by some sort of mechanical means, such as a tractor-drawn blade, and excess soil is gently shaked away. Plants can be inspected at this stage and those with diseased or damaged roots can be discarded or root pruned. Plants with large root systems are sometimes pruned to promote ease of handling.

Plants that are to be replanted fairly quickly can be bunched together in bundles of ten or more to assist ease of handling. Those plants that are to have an indefinite time before replanting (e.g. plants sold to retail nurseries) should have their roots protected to prevent them drying out. Materials such as moist sawdust can be packed around the roots to provide temporary protection.

Growing on

As the plants grow into a saleable size they must be protected from harsh environments, and the ravages of pests and diseases. Careful consideration must be also be given to where the containers are placed. The growing-on areas should be relatively level (no more than a 1:200 slope) for ease of access and handling and display of plants, but well drained with a clean surface below the plants. Concrete or asphalt are ideal surfacing materials. A thick layer of 1-2 cm diameter crushed rock is also good.

Woodshavings or other organic mulches are cheap and can be used with many types of plants, but they are not the ideal surface. In many cases the roots will grow down into the organic mulch, making the containers difficult to lift. The organic mulches may also draw down nitrogen from the medium in the containers as the mulch decomposes. It is also best to avoid plastic mulch lying on bare earth.

Watering, fertilising, regular spraying, pruning, staking and anything else needed to bring the plant to a marketable size are all important components of this stage of production.

Spacing

Plants in containers can be placed close together (maximising the number of plants which you can put into an area) or left with gaps between the containers. If plants are close, they compete for light and space. Taller plants may create shaded areas, stop water from getting to smaller plants, and prevent liquid feed reaching the lower plants. However, they may provide some protection from the elements for shorter plants.

Greater uniformity of growth (and general health) can be achieved by increased spacing, however, these benefits must be balanced against the increased area required. In hot humid climates, spacing may be essential with some plants to ensure adequate ventilation (i.e. air movement) around the plants to prevent diseases developing.

Staking

Plant growth can, in many instances, be controlled by staking. Staking young trees tends to promote top growth. However, if the trees are staked for too long (several years), the strength of the trunk and its ability to support a heavy crown can suffer.

Staked trees generally grow taller, but produce trunks which have a smaller diameter, and less taper. Creepers/climbers need to be staked for control.

Well spaced containers generally produce better shaped plants. Weed mat under the containers controls weeds and reduces pest and disease problems.

In-ground Production

A well structured, fertile soil is fundamental to successful in-ground production. However, even the best soils will soon diminish in quality (and quantity) as successive crops of plants are grown. An understanding of soils, including improvement techniques and testing procedures, will help the manager to prevent soil decline which will affect plant growth.

Soil provides plants with the following:

- Nutrition — the plant derives much of its food from nutrients in the soil.
- Support — the soil holds the plant firm and stops it falling over.
- Water and air — the roots absorb both water and air. The soil must contain both. A soil with too much air leaves the plant starved for water. A soil with too much water leaves the plant starved for air.

Different soils have different characteristics with respect to the above factors. For example, a sandy soil provides less support than a clay soil. A clay soil generally provides less air, but has a greater capacity to hold water than sand. An organic soil usually has a good ability to hold water, but doesn't always provide good support.

Naming the Soil

Soils are usually named according to texture. The following simple system can be used to broadly classify soils:

Place a small quantity of soil in the palm of your hand and add just enough water to make it plastic. Does it:

1. Stain your fingers   Yes or No?
2. Bind together   Yes or No?
3. Feel gritty   Yes or No?
4. Feel silky or sticky   Yes or No?
5. Make water cloudy   Yes or No?

The following soil types will typically give the following answers:

	1.	2.	3.	4.	5.
Sand	No	No	Yes	No	No
Sandy loam	No	Yes	Yes	No	No
Loam (or silt)	No	Yes	No	No	No
Clay loam	Yes	Yes	No	No	Yes
Clay	Yes	Yes	No	Yes	Yes

You should also be able to distinguish whether it is a coarse sand, medium sand, fine sand or very fine sand by the amount of grittiness. You can also find varying grades of other soil types by how well they bind together. For example, a clay will bind so tightly that it can be rolled into a ball and formed into shapes (just like potters' clay).

Organic soils have a large proportion of organic matter (more than 25%). These are usually black or brown in colour and feel silky. It is possible to get organic types of all of the above soils. Also, these soil types may be distinguished from others by placing a small amount in a glass of water. If most of it floats on top, then it is likely to be an organic soil.

Soil Structure

Good structure in a soil means that the mineral particles in the soil are bound together in crumbs (known as peds) of various sizes which are loosely arranged into larger groupings. This gives a well-structured soil a crumbly feel or appearance and provides plenty of pore spaces between the crumbs which allow good water penetration (infiltration), good aeration, and ease of penetration for plant roots (and other soil life).

Crumb formation can be enhanced by the addition of organic matter, some clay (in low clay soils), iron and aluminium (for soils low in these elements), and exchangeable calcium (usually applied as lime or gypsum).

Crumb formation is decreased with increasing levels of exchangeable sodium, which is common in areas with salinity problems. Soil structure can also be readily damaged by over-cultivation or poor cultivation techniques (particularly when the soil is very wet), by compaction (e.g. repeated trafficking of machinery), and by destroying soil life with repeated applications of chemicals.

Pore Space in Soils and Growing Media
Aeration and drainage of a growing medium will depend on the amount of pore space available in the growing medium. The pore space can be defined as the percentage of the volume of the media that

is not filled with solids. For example, a total pore space of 50% means that in every litre of medium there is 50% air and 50% solids. Total pore space can vary from as low as 30% in a heavily compacted soil, up to 95% in some types of peat. Good garden soils contain about 50% total pore space while good potting mixes and propagating media may have up to 60-80% total pore space.

Pore shape and size are also important. Large round or irregularly shaped particles result in bigger air spaces than flat or small particles. Large pore spaces allow greater movement of air and water. However, if the medium has a large proportion of large pore spaces then the water-holding capacity of the media will be poor. The ideal situation is where you have a combination of small and large pores to provide good aeration and drainage, as well as good water retention.

Drainage

One simple way of testing a soil's drainage properties is to observe the way in which water moves through soil when the soil is placed in a pot and watered. However, when soil is disturbed by digging its characteristics may change. A more reliable result can be obtained by inserting an empty tin can into the soil. With both the top and bottom removed, the can forms a parallel-sided tube which can be pushed into the soil to remove a relatively undisturbed soil sample. Be careful not to rock the can from side to side as you lift it from the soil as this will create a gap between the soil sample and the sides of the can. If you can remove the soil surrounding the can, and carefully slide a sharp flat blade or similar object under the can you will be able to minimise disturbance of the soil in the can. Leave a little room at the top of the can to hold water, add some water to see how it drains and then saturate the soil and add some more water to the top. You will often note slower drainage on saturated soil.

Observations can also be made in the field after rainfall or irrigation has occurred. Simply take note of how quickly water infiltrates into the soil, how much surface runoff occurs, and places (depressions) where water sits for any length of time.

Soil pH

This is a measure of the number of hydrogen (H+) ions present in a particular media (e.g. soils or potting media). These H+ ions are mainly caused by aluminium from soil colloids reacting with water to produce free hydrogen ions and hydroxyl (OH-) aluminium compounds.

The pH of a soil is measured using a logarithmic scale from 1 to 14, with 7 being neutral, above 7 considered alkaline, and below 7 acid. A one unit pH change means a ten-fold change in the acidity or alkalinity of the medium; for example a soil with a pH of 4 is ten times more acidic than one with a pH of 5, and 100 times more acidic than a soil with a pH of 6. For most soils, the pH can range from around 3.8 to 8.2, depending on the cations present. The pH of a growing medium will have an effect on the amounts of nutrients available for plant growth.

Plant species differ in the pH range they can tolerate. Most plants prefer a pH in the range of 5.5 to 7.5. It is in this range that most nutrient elements are available for plant growth. Outside of this range elements (e.g. phosphorus) may become insoluble (known as 'locked') in the soil and unavailable to plants, or elements, such as aluminium and manganese become so soluble that they are toxic to plant growth. In very acid soils, the activities of the following soil organisms are reduced:

- nitrogen-fixing bacteria
- bacteria that convert ammonium to nitrate
- organisms that break down organic matter

Also, in highly acid soil, various agricultural chemicals (herbicides and nematicides) are not effective.

Testing pH

Soil pH can be simply measured using either liquids or papers (i.e. litmus) that change colour according to the pH of the medium being tested. It can also be measured using electronic meters. These will be more expensive to purchase than indicator liquids or papers, but they are cheap to run, quick and easy to use, and depending on the type purchased, give very accurate results.

Soil Nutrition

More than fifty elements are known to be used by plants, in varying amounts. At least sixteen are used by all plants. The nine nutrient elements generally used by plants in the largest quantities are carbon (C), hydrogen (H) and oxygen (O), which are obtained from air and water; and nitrogen (N), phosphorus (P), potassium (K), calcium (Ca), magnesium (Mg) and sulphur (S) which are derived principally from the soil or growing media. These are sometimes known as the major elements. It is the NPK elements that are most widely used in fertilisers.

Carbon, hydrogen and oxygen are readily obtained from air and water, while calcium, magnesium and sulphur are generally present in sufficient quantities in soils to maintain good plant growth.

The remaining elements are known as the micronutrients, or trace elements. They are just as necessary for plant growth as the major elements, but in much smaller quantities. Examples are copper (Cu), molybdenum (Mo), cobalt (Co), zinc (Zn), manganese (Mn), iron (Fe) and boron (B). Some soils, particularly leached ones, may be deficient in one or more trace elements. Often one application of a fertiliser containing the required trace element is sufficient to ensure adequate supplies of that nutrient for years.

Soil nutrition is (to some extent) indicated by the vigour of plants growing in a soil. Simple soil test kits can also be used to give approximate levels of nitrogen, potassium and phosphorus. More comprehensive and accurate soil analysis can be carried out by soil laboratory services.

Improving soils

Ways to improve soils include:
• Adding sand to clay soils to improve drainage. This usually requires substantial amounts of sand, and it must be well mixed to have a beneficial effect.
• Adding clay to sandy soil to improve its ability to hold water.
• Adding organic matter to any but very organic soils. While improving soil water-holding capacity, it will not affect drainage to the same degree as the addition of clay will.
• Adding organic matter will usually improve the nutritional status of the soil.
• Use of soil ameliorants:
— Lime to reduce acidity and help improve soil structure
— Gypsum to help improve soil structure of clayish soils
— Wetting agents to help water penetration in sandy and highly organic soils
• Crop rotations.
• Good cultivation techniques.
• Growing legumes as a cover crop to help 'fix' nitrogen into the soil.
• Surface working of the soil surface (e.g. mounding, ridging, laser grading, terracing) to improve surface drainage or reduce erosion.

Organic matter

Organic matter is very important in improving and maintaining soils for the following reasons:
• To promote the formation of a crumbly soil structure.
• As a source of nutrients for plant and animal growth.
• To act as a buffer against extremes of temperature or chemical changes in the soil.
• To improve soil moisture retention.

The average mineral soil contains around 2–5% organic matter. The soil's organic content will drop if you remove plant material which grows in a soil (e.g. a crop) and don't return an equivalent amount of organic material to the soil. The soil's organic content is restored or increased in the following ways:
• Regular additions of compost.
• Use of organic mulches on the soil surface.
• Feeding plants with manure (preferably well rotted).
• Growing green manure crops and cultivating the crop into the soil or mulching onto the soil surface.

Laboratory testing of soils

There are many sophisticated tests which can be carried out to determine the soil's chemical and physical characteristics. These tests generally require expensive laboratory equipment which is beyond the means of the average nursery. There are, however, laboratories in most major cities which will conduct the tests for you.

Taking a soil sample for testing:
• Take samples from soil mix stockpiles before adding fertiliser.
• Take samples from soil in beds prior to seeding or planting.
• Take samples from soil in pots from top and bottom of several different pots.
• Wait at least 6 hours after watering (or rain) before taking a sample.
• If dry fertiliser has been used, wait at least 5 days after application before sampling.
• If liquid fertiliser has been used, wait at least 48 hours before sampling.
• Remove mulch from surface and the top 1 cm before sampling.
• Use a soil auger, corer or some similar device for taking samples to ensure a sample across the total profile of the soil. The soil sample to be analysed should be representative of the area.

Using a conductivity meter
This is a small electronic device used to measure the flow of electricity through water, potting media or soil. When mineral ions are present (e.g. nutrients from fertilisers) electric currents will flow faster. The more mineral ions present, the faster the electric current. The meter will then give a higher reading.

By testing soil or media regularly it is easy to determine if there are too many toxins present, if salt residues from fertilisers are too high, or if fertiliser levels are too low. They are also useful for keeping a check on water quality. Conductivity meters are relatively inexpensive, and can be an extremely useful tool if used frequently and correctly.

Toxins
Toxins that damage plant growth can occur through the build-up of excess salts in growing media, from overuse or build-up of chemicals such as pesticides, and from chemicals found in uncomposted woodchips or shavings used for growing media — particularly those of *Pinus* and *Eucalyptus* species. The following simple test can often remove any doubts about whether a growing media is safe to use.

Radish test for toxins:
1. Place the growing mix in a pot.
2. Sow several radish seeds.
3. When the radish seeds are at a developed two-leaf stage, remove some seedlings carefully, and wash the mix from the roots.
4. If the extreme tip of the root is a dark colour, it is likely that there are toxins in the mix.

Flow Charts

To gain a better understanding of the procedures involved in production it is helpful to produce an operational flow chart which outlines the various steps undertaken in each of the four stages of production.

An example of a flow chart for propagating eucalypts grown from seed is presented below:

Propagation stage
1. Obtain seed
2. Mix propagating medium
3. Sterilise propagating medium (if applicable)
4. Fill seed tray
5. Water tray
6. Sow seed
7. Cover seed
8. Water seed trays
9. Place trays in propagation area (e.g. glasshouse) Germination takes place

Transplanting stage
1. Mix growing media or purchase soil mix
2. Sterilise media
3. Bring seedlings and soil mix to potting area
4. Transplant seedlings into pots or tubes
5. Move potted plants to protected or semi-protected position for growing on (e.g. shaded position)

Growing-on stage
1. Mix and sterilise/or buy potting soil
2. Bring soil and plants together in potting area
3. Pot up into container which plant will be sold in
4. Allow growth to full size (apply fertiliser and water, prune, etc. as needed)

Marketing stage
1. Prepare and label for sales
2. Load into van
3. Call on retail nurseries canvassing sales
4. Unload plants as they sell

Note: The above example is only one method by which eucalypts might be produced and marketed by a nursery. Irrespective of the method you follow, you should seek to make a critical evaluation of your efficiencies. Try to discover places where your operation can be streamlined. Can you save time (or money) by doing anything differently to the way it is done now? For example, perhaps you can eliminate mixing of medium by purchasing a media which is premixed, or perhaps potting up can be eliminated by direct seeding into the container which you will sell the plant in.

The flow chart can be expanded to include a column that lists the hours spent on each task. This can be used to determine which tasks are the most time-consuming, how much each task is costing you in terms of labour, and specific labour requirements for each task. From this you can determine the most efficient use of your labour force (e.g. when to hire casual staff; planning tasks so that you don't have a lot of work one week and very little the next; allocating the most suitable employee to each task).

The Marketing Stage

Once the plant has grown to a marketable size, it then needs to be packaged and presented for sale. The marketing stage involves a lot more than just selling. Some nurseries devote staff exclusively to marketing tasks other than sales (e.g. selecting and compiling orders, labelling, packaging, and loading stock onto trucks).

4 Managing Plants in the Nursery

A significant part of nursery work is simply keeping plants alive and healthy. The biggest and healthiest plants are inevitably the ones customers prefer to buy. Healthy plants will also reach a saleable size a lot quicker than those which are stressed by pest and disease problems, or by poor watering and nutrition.

Managing Plants in Production/Propagation Nurseries

Propagation nurseries *must* have a reliable supply of good quality propagation material. This might be seed from reliable seed suppliers or plants which can readily be used as a source for seed collecting. It might also be cutting or grafting material from healthy, correctly identified plants (i.e. 'known varieties'). Plants which are used as a source of propagating material are called 'stock plants'.

Stock plants might or might not be on the nursery site, but ideally they should be in a convenient and accessible location. They are extremely important to a nursery's operation, and establishing a reliable source of stock plants can be one of the nurseryperson's biggest problems.

The quality of the stock plants is perhaps the biggest influence upon everything which happens later in a nursery. If stock plants are in poor condition:

- cuttings or grafts may have a lower rate of success.
- cuttings may be slower to form roots, and grafts slower to grow together.
- pest or disease problems can be transmitted from stock plants to other plants in the propagation area or greenhouse.
- new plants might not develop as strongly as those taken from healthy, vigorous stock.

Selecting Stock Plants

Only use:
- plants free of disease and pests.
- plants which are true to type.
- plants which have been grown in optimum conditions.
- plants which have been growing well.
- plants which have been adequately fed, and are free from signs of any nutrient deficiency or leaf burn.

Sources of stock plants

It's nearly always best to grow stock plants on the nursery site. This means that they are immediately accessible, maintenance can be easily carried out, and cutting material can be taken when it best suits the nursery's requirements. Sometimes, however, there isn't sufficient room at the nursery, or the growing environment is not suitable. When grown on the nursery site, avoid giving the stock plants second rate positions. They should never be grown in places which are 'no good for anything else'.

Some nurseries grow their stock plants in rows in a special paddock. The plants are well fertilised, well watered, and given the best of care in every possible way. Other nurseries grow stock plants in large containers in premium potting medium, and once again, the plants are given extra special care.

Nursery plants are also frequently used to supply propagation material (i.e. plants which are to eventually be sold are pruned to supply cuttings). This can supply a significant amount of material in some cases, but pruning must be carefully done to avoid destroying the shape or general health of plants which are destined for market.

Sometimes permission can be obtained to collect material from public gardens (e.g. botanic gardens), parks, commercial properties and roadside plantings. It may be necessary to offer something in return — perhaps exchanging these rights for some free plants.

Private gardens can also be a source of material, but the difficulty is often discovering what exists close to the nursery. By joining local garden clubs a nurseryperson can sometimes establish a source of propagation material, and at the same time develop goodwill for the nursery in the local area.

Native plants can sometimes be collected from public bushland, but there are legal restrictions on what you are allowed to do. These should be checked out fully before collecting *any* propagating material.

If collecting from properties not owned by the nursery, it is important not to abuse the privilege and risk not being able to collect in future. Be polite and friendly to owners, employees or caretakers of properties you collect from and their cooperation in the future will be invaluable.

Planting out stock plants

Stock plants should always be planted and maintained in the very best conditions. Factors such as aspect, amount of light received, and soil conditions should be considered carefully. The area to be planted should be cleaned thoroughly before planting, with all weeds and rubbish removed. Ideally the soil should be sterilised. Methyl bromide has been widely used but is now banned in some places. Solarisation or steam can be used if you prefer to avoid chemicals.

Stock plants should be kept apart from the main production area of a nursery, so that disease or pest problems in the nursery can be stopped before they infect the stock area.

Labelling Stock Plants

Incorrectly labelled plants are a major problem in many nurseries. If a customer is paying for a particular variety of plant, then they should be assured of getting a plant of that variety. Selection of a 'true to type' cultivar is something which often requires expert knowledge. If there is the slightest doubt about the identity of any stock plant, then don't propagate from it until it has been identified by an expert, such as a botanist experienced in plant taxonomy. Many botanical gardens or herbariums will identify plants for you. Some will do it for free, others may charge a small fee.

Cross check spelling with a reputable publication such as the *Royal Horticultural Society Dictionary* or *Hortus Third*. If in doubt, contact a herbarium (usually attached to botanic gardens) to double check the spelling. Do not assume that a label supplier has the correct spelling.

Make sure that any labels used are durable, and that information on them can be clearly read. It is also a good idea to keep a record book or map in a secure place that includes as much information as possible about each stock plant. Details recorded can include the original source of the plant, who identified it, maintenance details, and when and how much cutting material is taken. This provides a good back-up in case of lost or damaged labels, and if doubts are raised about the identity of propagated plants.

Maintaining stock plants

Pruning may be necessary to control the type of growth as well as the size and shape of the plant. Pruning a few months prior to taking cuttings can stimulate more growth of the type which is best suited for cuttings. Feeding should be adequate, but be careful — too much nitrogen can stimulate too much soft, weak growth.

Some types of plants (e.g. those grown from cuttings) may require very hard annual pruning to encourage suitable cutting material to be developed for the next season.

Collecting propagating material

It is essential to keep propagating material as fresh and healthy as possible between the time it is collected and when it is used. The best way to do this is to collect it immediately before you are about to use it. Dormant vegetation will be very slow to deteriorate, but some material can deteriorate within a matter of hours (e.g. seeds or cuttings from some rainforest plants).

Cutting or grafting material collected for propagation is generally best placed in a plastic bag, perhaps with a little moist sphagnum moss, and put in a cool place (e.g. in an insulated box or car fridge) until it is to be used. Sometimes material is collected, stood in buckets of water and placed in a cool area (e.g. under a bench). Material that is not going to be used immediately can often be stored in a refrigerator (not in the freezer section) for a week, sometimes longer, before being used.

Sources of seed

Nurseries can generally grow plants more easily and cheaply by seed than by any other technique. Plants grown from seed, however, will often vary considerably in their characteristics; for example, some plants might grow stronger or taller than others, be more susceptible to disease, or have different coloured flowers. Nevertheless, a wide range of plants are grown by seed including most bedding plants, vegetables, farm and forestry trees, and many rootstocks for fruit and deciduous ornamental trees. The problems of seedling variation can be minimised by paying particular attention to the source of seed, and to how the seed is treated both in storage and in the propagation process.

The source of seed is very important with regard to quality. Some seed suppliers do not supply pure seed. Rubbish or weed seeds may be mixed with the seed, or the seed may be infested with pests and/or diseases.

The time of seed harvesting and the health of the parent stock are also important factors. The percentage viability of the batch may be reduced if seeds are collected before they have properly developed, and the vigour of the seedlings may be low if the seeds were not collected from strong and healthy plants.

There are four main sources of seed:

1. Seed collected from the wild

Seed collected from plants growing in their natural habitat is less likely to be cross pollinated by plants from other provenances, and you can be more certain of where it came from and how it will grow than if you had purchased it from a seed supplier.

2. Seed exchanges

Many botanic gardens operate seed exchange programs, where they produce annual seed lists and swap seed with other people involved in the program. Such programs are particularly valuable as a source of more scarce varieties of plants. Some horticultural associations and societies also operate seed banks for their members.

3. Commercial seed suppliers

There are many thousands of seed companies operating throughout the world. Some breed new varieties of plants and grow seed crops to harvest. Others buy seed from collectors (who collect from the wild or from gardens).

Major problems of using this source include:
• Collectors identifying seed source plants incorrectly.
• Unreliable supply (if they can't supply, it's too late for you to collect for yourself).
• Uncertainty about the quality.
• Developing a dependence on the supplier.

Major advantages of using this source include:
• Convenience.
• Obtaining a seed source for plants which do not set seed well locally.
• Savings on labour costs.

4. Collecting seed yourself locally

You, or your representative, might collect seed from plants on your property, or other nearby properties as it matures throughout the year. Seed may also be collected from public parks and gardens or private gardens (with permission).

The major advantages of this source are:
• You have a greater degree of control over collection, storage and treatment techniques.
• You can be sure you have got exactly what you want.
• You learn a lot more about the plants you are growing because you see them in their mature state.

A simple 'spine' nursery layout with one main road running through the centre of the nursery. Protected growing areas are on one side of the road, and hardening off (exposed) growing areas are on the other side. This layout provides easy access for vehicles and minimises handling and movement of plants. (Bau Farm Nursery, Alstonville, northern NSW)

Flat ground is preferable for setting up a nursery. Sloping sites may require terracing, which increases establishment costs.

In early winter deciduous grafted trees are dug up from nursery rows, placed in bundles, then heeled in prior to despatch to buyers such as retailers and orchardists.

In-ground production of orchids. The orchids are growing in beds of gravel under shadecloth. (Wonga Belle Orchid Nursery and Flower Farm, Far North Queensland)

Eucalypts grown in black plastic tubes (flexible bags). Seeds are germinated in trays filled with a sand/peat mix. The seedlings are then separated and planted into the tubes. The depth of the container ensures the plant will develop a strong root system, and the narrow diameter allows a greater number of plants to be grown in a given space. This production method is ideal for producing large numbers of plants for farm planting, roadside planting, forestry and other applications where mass planting is to be done at minimal cost.

Stock plant bed. Healthy plants grown at the nursery site make the job of obtaining quality cutting material more convenient and cost effective. (Canning Nursery, Perth, Western Australia)

- You can save on the cost of purchasing seed (although collecting can be time consuming, particularly if you have to travel to collection sites).

Major disadvantages are that the amount of seed available to harvest may vary considerably from year to year, and you are 'tied' to the particular time when the seed is ready to harvest. This means that you may have to stop other tasks while you go and collect seeds.

Gene pool/provenance

The place which a particular plant originated from gives it a range of genetic characteristics which are very specific to that batch of seeds. For example, *Eucalyptus camaldulensis* seed from one stand of trees might be very tolerant of salt, while seed from another stand of *Eucalyptus camaldulensis* might not tolerate salt at all. This characteristic is known as the seed's 'provenance'.

Storing seed

Seeds are alive and like any living thing they can be harmed by adverse conditions. Seeds of some species do not store for very long at all and in these cases propagation should be done with fresh seed only (this group includes many spring ripening seeds of temperate zone plants). Most seeds, however, will store for at least six months without loss of viability, provided optimum environmental storage conditions are provided.

Factors affecting storage of seed

Moisture Content

Many short-lived seeds lose viability if they become dry (e.g. citrus seed only withstand slight drying). On the other hand, medium to long-lived seeds need to be dry to survive long periods of storage (4–6% moisture level is ideal — higher or lower can be detrimental to viability). For seeds not adversely affected by low moisture, each 1% decrease in seed moisture between 5% and 14% doubles the life of the seed.

Fluctuations in moisture levels during storage will reduce longevity; for this reason, seeds keep better in dry climates than in areas of high humidity.

Temperature

Most seeds will store for longer periods at lower temperatures. Each decrease of 4.6°C (9°F) between 0°C and 44°C (32°F and 112°F) will double seed storage life.

Storage Atmosphere

Some techniques of modifying gas levels (e.g. increasing carbon dioxide) can be of value.

Difficult seeds

Some types of seeds are much more difficult to germinate than others. In their natural state most plants have adopted mechanisms which allow germination to occur with relative ease. For many 'difficult to germinate seeds', it is possible to carry out a pregermination treatment which will increase the chances of success.

Types of seed storage

Open storage

Seeds of many annuals, perennials, vegetables and cereals can be successfully stored in bins, sacks or paper bags. Apart from a few exceptions (e.g. corn, onion, parsley, parsnip, delphinium, kochia and candytuft), seeds from these groups will normally retain viability for at least a few years. Fumigation or insecticide/fungicide applications are sometimes necessary.

Cold storage with or without humidity control

Temperatures below 10°C will improve the longevity of virtually any type of seed. Cold storage of tree and shrub seed is recommended if the seed is to be held for more than one year.

Cold moist storage

Some seed should be stored between 2°C and 10°C in a container which contains some moisture-retaining material (e.g. peat or sphagnum moss). Relative humidity should be 80–90%. Examples of species requiring this type of storage are *Acer saccharinum, Carya, Castanea, Corylus, Citrus, Eriobytra* (loquat), *Fagus, Juglans, Litchi, Persea* (avocado) and *Quercus*.

Dormancy factors affecting germination

Physical dormancy

Seed coats, and sometimes hardened sections of other parts of the seed, become impermeable to water. In the natural environment these hard layers are softened by environmental effects such as freezing and thawing, mechanical abrasion, and attack by micro organisms. This condition is characteristic of many plant families, including Mimosaceae, Papilionaceae, Caesalpinaceae, Malvaceae, Geraniaceae and Solanaceae.

Mechanical dormancy
The seed covering is too hard to allow the embryo to expand when germinating, e.g. a peach stone.

Chemical dormancy
Chemicals in the seed may inhibit germination. This is common with fleshy fruits and berries. Seeds of this type usually need to be removed from the fruit and washed before sowing.

Morphological dormancy
In some seeds, the seed is not fully developed at the time the fruit ripens and it needs time before it can be sown. This is common in the Araliaceae, Ranunculaceae, Ericaceae, Primulaceae and Apiaceae families

Internal dormancy
There are a number of types of dormancy where germination is controlled by the internal condition of the seed. The most significant example is moist chilling, where the seed needs to go through a period of cold temperatures before it will germinate. This is common in the Rosaceae family.

Testing for seed viability using the viability test
In this test a colourless liquid is imbibed in the seed. The liquid reacts with living tissue and produces a red substance which cannot be diffused — hence any living parts of the seed turn red or pink, and any dead parts of the seed remain unchanged. The chemical used is a 1% solution of 2.3.5.-triphenyltetrazolium chloride (or bromide).

This test is conducted by cutting a seed in half so that the embryo can be seen. The seed is then soaked in the solution for 12 hours in the dark at a temperature between 20°C and 30°C (in some cases 24 hours is needed). The seed is then studied (a hand lens may be necessary). Seeds can be selected at random from a batch and tested to give an indication of overall viability.

Managing Plants in Retail Nurseries

A retail nursery needs to keep plants looking at their peak all of the time. Plants are bought into a retail nursery from a different environment, sometimes following a long trip on a truck. These things stress the plant, and it is only natural for a plant to deteriorate a little when it is first bought into a retail environment. This deterioration may only be mild, and it may take days or even weeks to become visible, depending on such things as the type of plant and time of year. Nurseries with a high turnover rate which can sell plants fast do not have such a problem with plants deteriorating. For other retail nurseries, life can be a constant battle to keep the plants looking good.

Routine jobs should include:
- Daily inspection of a selection of individual plants (check for over watering, under watering, disease, pests, sunburn, need for repotting, etc).
- Removing spent (dead) flowers.
- Removing damaged or marked leaves.
- Pruning to shape.
- Moving overcrowded pots to allow better ventilation and light penetration.
- Removing sick plants to an out of sight 'hospital' area.
- Rearranging plants to draw the customer's attention to the healthiest and most attractive plants, as well as those plants in flower.
- Moving out of season stock away from sales areas.
- Moving seasonal stock into prominence.
- Moving plants into protected areas when weather changes.
- Potting up pot bound plants.
- Routine fertilising.
- Routine spraying for weeds, pests and diseases.
- Maintaining good hygiene/cleanliness.

It is particularly important to respond to problems detected in inspections immediately.

How to conduct a plant inspection

When a plant becomes 'sick', the cause could be one or several things. More often than not, there are several factors involved; for example, minor diseases or environmental problems weaken the plant, making it more susceptible to a more damaging (obvious) disorder.

When you inspect a plant for problems, you need to systematically consider all of the things which might possibly be going wrong.

First Systematically examine the plant and take note of any abnormalities. Look at the leaves:
Are there abnormal markings, swellings or distortion?
Is there any discolouration?
Are there dead patches or holes?

Look at the fruit and flowers:
Are the flowers and fruit developing well?
Is there any fruit drop?
Is fruit undersized?

Look at the stems/branches:
Are the growth tips lush and growing fast? (A healthy plant will have lush, growing tips. If other parts are damaged but the tips are lush, this can indicate that the plant is recovering from a previous problem).
Are there any abnormalities on the stems?

Look at the roots:
Are the root tips well formed and healthy or black and rotting?
Are the roots strong or is the plant loose in the ground?
Are roots growing on the surface of the soil? This may indicate the soil is infertile or dry deep down and the roots are coming up for water and nutrients.

What parts of the plant are most damaged?
The parts which are most exposed to the problem will be most affected. For example:
• frost damage occurs more on parts most exposed to frost;
• sun burn is more likely to occur on those parts exposed to the sun, as well as on new soft growth;
• fruit rots may occur on branches close to the ground where disease spores can splash up from the soil;
• small animals tend to eat lush growth in preference to older tough foliage, while grazing animals will eat lower growth on shrubs and trees that is within their reach.

Second Examine the surroundings and note anything which may relate to abnormalities noticed when you examined the plant.

Soil:
Is it wet or dry?
Is it well drained?

Surrounding plants:
Are they healthy or are they displaying similar symptoms?

Environment:
Consider exposure to wind, frost, sun and excessive shade.
Has anything been changed since the problem arose? For example, a building or large tree which provided protection may have been removed.
Is the plant at the bottom of a hill or slope? Could something have washed down from further up the hill (e.g. a weedicide, or disease spores from another plant)?

Third Decide, based on the information collected, which group you think the main problem comes from: pest, disease, nutrition, environment or weed. Decide whether it is likely if there is more than one major problem. Eliminate the groups you can.

Fourth Select a suitable control method or methods. The following table may also give you some clues to possible causes of plant disorders.

Diagnosis of Plant Disorders

Symptom	Possible Causes	Treatment
Spindly growth	Low light (e.g. shade); excess water; high temperatures; plants too close together	Improve light; reduce watering; reduce night temperature in greenhouse by cooling or ventilation; reduce feeding; increase spacing between plants.
Growth reduced	Insufficient nutrient and/or water	Feed more often but in low concentration; water more often.
Old or lower leaves yellowing	Nitrogen deficiency	Feed the plant/s with a fertiliser high in nitrogen. A highly soluble or liquid fertiliser will give quick results. This can be followed up with a slow release nitrogen fertiliser or further applications of highly soluble forms.

Young leaves yellowing between veins	Iron deficiency	Similar treatment as for nitrogen above.
Purple leaves	Phosphorus deficiency	Similar treatment to nitrogen.
Root tips burnt or discoloured on container-grown plants	Excess fertiliser or salts, or toxic chemicals in soils or potting mixes (sometimes occurs when media is fresh)	Leach media thoroughly to wash away excess nutrient or toxin or repot into potting mix with low salt/toxin levels.
Woody growth	Plants overhardened (i.e. exposed to too tough conditions), or slow growing	Increase feeding; if problem is excessive, also prune to promote a new flush of growth.
Stems very wet and decaying at base of the plant	Damping off disease caused by dirty conditions, high humidity and/or overcrowding	Thin out plants; apply fungicide.
Algae, moss or liverwort on surface of soils and potting mixes	Excess moisture and nutrient on surface. Doesn't harm plant initially but can impair flow of nutrient solution in the long term	Reduce watering; increase ventilation; use better draining medium; some chemicals (e.g. ferrous sulphate) can be used to kill algae and moss.
Poor root growth	Poor aeration or drainage in medium; low temperature in medium; toxic chemical in medium	Determine which of these is the problem and act accordingly.

Practical Exercise

Nursery Inspection Sheet

It can be a useful exercise to develop a checklist or inspection sheet for nursery staff to use when undertaking routine inspections for pest and disease problems.

Most nurseries are divided into several sections (propagation area, shadehouse, greenhouse, etc.),

and a separate inspection sheet should be filled out for each section. The following is an example of one such sheet. The nursery manager may decide to establish a procedure where this sheet is used daily or weekly in order to determine whether any pest, disease or other problems are developing and need attention. This can be an excellent time saver for the manager, allowing a clear picture of the current status of the nursery to be determined quickly and efficiently.

NURSERY NAME: . . . .

INSPECTION DATE: . . . .

INSPECTION CARRIED OUT BY: . . . .

NURSERY SECTION: . . . .

OVERALL CONDITION OF PLANTS

Very Healthy. . . . Healthy. . . . Medium Health . . . . Sick . . . . Very Sick . . . . Dead . . . .

Condition of the Worst Plants
Very Healthy. . . . Healthy. . . . Medium Health . . . . Sick . . . . Very Sick . . . . Dead . . . .

ROOT INSPECTION
Expose some of the roots on at least two different plants by either digging into the soil or partly removing the plant from the pot.
Root tips: White, healthy and growing . . . .
Darkened or discoloured . . . . Rotting or dead . . . . Pot bound . . . . Roots needing water . . . Roots too wet . . . Roots very hot . . . . Roots eaten, chewed or damaged by insects or other animals . . . . Roots or soil contains pests (give description . . . .
. . . .)
Roots or soil contains fungal or some other growth (give description . . . .)

FOLIAGE
Growing tips: Lush, rapid growth . . . Healthy but not lush . . . . Discoloured . . . . Looks sick . . . .
Older leaves: Lush, very healthy . . .
Damaged . . . Discoloured . . . Has dead

spots... Some dropping...
General foliage: Thick... Sparse...
Hardened... Soft/Tender... Balanced
shape... Poor shape....

SPECIFIC PROBLEMS DETECTED

List the names of any insects, diseases or other
specific problems which are detected and
identified:

. . . .

NEEDS TO BE DONE

Procedure	Plant Variety Concerned	Procedure	Plant Variety Concerned
Staking	. . . .	Move to greenhouse	. . . .
Pruning	. . . .	Move to shadehouse	. . . .
Re-label	. . . .	Move to	. . . .
Feeding	. . . . . .	Watering	. . . .

RECOMMENDATIONS

To be done urgently: . . . .
To be done, but not urgent: . . . .

Controlling Pests and Diseases in the Nursery

The main ways of controlling pests and diseases are
through:
1. Hygiene or cleanliness
2. Resistant plant varieties
3. Biological controls
4. Soil drenches/dips
5. Chemical controls (artificial and naturally
derived)
6. Physical control methods — mowing, slashing,
burning, hand removal, physical barriers (netting
and fences)

The easiest way to control pests and diseases is to
avoid ever getting these problems in the first place.
There are two main ways of doing this. One is to
practise hygiene, and this is something every nursery
should and could do. The other is to avoid growing
plants which have pest or disease problems. This is
not always easy as many of the popular plants are
prone to pest and disease attack.

Hygiene

Pests and diseases can spread many different ways
including the following:
• dipping healthy cuttings in hormone or water in
which diseased material has been dipped.
• irrigation (from contaminated water sources) or
rainwater (dripping off structures or diseased plants,
or by splashing up soil).
• soil-borne diseases on the hose if it's dropped on
the ground.
• contaminated soil on the bottom of pots/trays.
• tools, clothes, shoes and workers' hands.
• contaminated soil mixes or pots.
• infected plant material.

Rules for maintaining sanitation

• Treat all soil with either steam or chemical
fumigation, such as methyl bromide.
• Segregate clean and treated pots. Never store clean
pots on the ground. Clean all containers before use.
• Don't use/transplant diseased seedlings or
cuttings. Destroy infected material by burning).
• Use clean plant material from a specialist
propagator (i.e. if buying tubes to grow on, check
that they come from a clean nursery).
• Disinfect cutting material before using (e.g. dip
in a weak bleach solution).
• Take cuttings from top of plants as this is the
cleanest part.
• Sterilise tools before use — wash with Dettol,
formaldehyde, Biogram, bleach etc.
• Wash tools before using on a different plant.
• Place clean plant material on cleaned/sterilised
benches.
• Segregate propagation activities from sales/
growing on areas.
• Avoid handling treated soil unnecessarily.
• Don't handle soil or plants unless hands have been
washed with hot water and soap.
• Avoid splashing water near sterilised soil, pots,
benches, etc.
• Pots should always be placed on well-drained
surfaces — preferably concrete, asphalt or fibro
sheet/non corrosive metal for benches. Blue metal
or some other type of crushed rock is acceptable.
Trays should be set on bricks above the ground.
• Hang hoses on a hook — don't lie them on the
ground.
• Place any plants which you suspect to be diseased
in an isolated area.

• Apply control methods to pests and diseases as soon as they are detected to prevent their spread.

Common Insect Pests in the Nursery

If you think or know it's an insect but you're not sure what type it is, try to see how it feeds. The following list may assist in quick identification of insects damaging plants. They are grouped below according to the type of plant damage which they cause. The list is not exhaustive, but it should cover most common pests you will encounter.

Insects (and other pests) which chew above ground
Ants, Army worm, Bugs, Beetles, Caterpillars, Crickets, Cutworm, Earwig, Flea beetle, Grasshopper, Leafminer, Leafroller, Leaf skeletoniser, Sawfly, Slug, Snail, Springtail, Weevil

Insects (and other pests) which suck plant parts above ground
Aphis, Harlequin bug, Lace bug, Leafhopper, Mealy bug, Mite, Psyllid, Scale, Squash bug, Thrip, Tree hopper, Whitefly

Insects (and other pests) which feed below ground
Root aphis, Root nematodes, Root borer, Rootworm, Root weevil, Woolly aphis, Wireworm, Beetle larvae

Borers (including fruit borers)
Codling moth, Bark beetle, Corn earworm, White pine weevil, Melon worm, Longicorn beetle, European apple sawfly

Diseases

If your plant problem is a disease, in most cases it will be one of the following types of diseases:
• Anthracnose — dead spots, usually sunken
• Blight — quick death of plant parts
• Canker — dead tissue in one place only
• Damping off — rotting of young plants at soil level
• Galls — abnormal swellings
• Leaf Spot — dead or off colour spots on leaves
• Mildew — young growth becomes distorted and grey/white/powdery
• Rots — decaying tissue
• Rust — brown-orange spots or stripes

• Smut — sooty-powdery covering
• Sooty Mould — similar to smut (associated with insects)
• Virus — causes distortion or discolouration
• Wilt — drooping foliage

Biological Control of Pests and Diseases

Biocontrol is when we use living things such as predators or parasites to attack and harm pests and diseases. In the nursery industry the most widely used biocontrol methods are the release of predatory mites to control some pest mite species, in particular red spider mite, and the use of sprays containing *Bacillus thuringiensis* which specifically attacks caterpillars.

When the predatory mites are released, they should be distributed as evenly as possible, and watering should be avoided for at least 24 hours. In addition, the use of chemicals should be avoided for at least a few weeks after releasing the parasitic mites.

Other Non-chemical Controls

Some non-chemical controls can be very effective, but others only have a very mild effect and do not work significantly when used against an established problem in a nursery. Some methods are outlined below:

Traps
Yellow attracts some insects (e.g. Aphis). A yellow card coated with honey will attract aphis which can then become stuck to the card. Similarly, white sticky cards placed in an open sunny position will attract and trap thrips.

Physical barriers
Large animals such as rabbits, possums, deer or domestic grazing animals can be a very serious problem in some places. The most effective control of these pests is to fence or cage nursery areas.

Snails and slugs are deterred from crawling over surfaces which feel too rough to them. Woodshavings or diatomaceous earth can be used as a barrier against these pests.

Chemical Controls

Many nurseries use chemicals extensively to control pest and disease problems. These can be used either as part of a routine pest and disease control program, or as a solution to problems when they are detected.

Routine chemical programs can be a significant expense in a nursery, but they do ensure that stock looks good at all times, and that production schedules are not interrupted by unexpected infestations of insects or diseases. However, the regular use of chemicals does have a number of disadvantages. These include potential pollution of your property and surrounding areas, possible development of pesticide-resistant strains of pests and diseases, and health risks to staff and customers from poor pesticide storage, handling and use.

These problems can be minimised by careful selection of the chemicals used, and how and when they are used. Chemicals which persist in the environment for long periods (i.e. for years) are best avoided. By rotating a variety of different chemicals to treat the one problem, problems such as the compounding effect of individual chemicals building up in the environment, or encouraging pest resistance to develop, are minimised.

Safety precautions and recommendations given by pesticide manufacturers should always be thoroughly read and closely followed.

Nurseries can reduce their use of chemicals by only using them when a problem arises, but this technique will only work if routine daily inspections are made of plants to determine whether problems are developing and require attention. A nurseryperson needs to have a greater degree of expertise in diagnosing problems if this approach is to be successful, so it may involve spending more on wages to employ skilled staff or provide suitable training, however that expense can be offset by savings on chemicals.

Chemicals can be applied either as granules (sprinkled at the base of the plant), dusts (puffed or blowed onto plants), or as a liquid spray. Granules have a distinct advantage in that they are safer and are less likely to be absorbed into the human body. Sprays and dusts may drift in the breeze, thus wasting the chemical, and perhaps causing pollution, or spray damage to plants nearby.

The type of sprays used and the frequency recommended will differ from nursery to nursery depending on local conditions such as weather patterns, the types of problems which occur in the area, and on the types of plants being grown in that nursery.

Some nurseries use subcontractors to carry out the spraying. This works well for a routine spray program if the contractor is competent and reliable; but it is not usually appropriate for nurseries who only treat problems as they arise. Problems must be treated as soon as they are detected, and therefore the contractor must be available when the problem occurs. This can often be a problem, particularly if the contractor is in demand.

Pesticides and fungicides commonly used in nurseries

Chemical	Use	Comments
Benomyl (Benlate)	Broad spectrum, systemic fungicide, particularly used for damping off and powdery mildews. Used for soil/media drenches, foliar sprays and dusting seeds.	Do not get on skin; use gloves; can cause long-term health problems.
Dimethoate (Rogor)	Broad spectrum, systemic insecticide, particularly for sucking insects.	Highly toxic to bees.
Disulfoton (Di-Syston)	Broad spectrum, systemic insecticide and acaride.	Applied to soil. Very toxic, but granular form is relatively safe to use. Persists for many weeks in soils or plant tissue.
Furalaxyl (Fongarid)	Used for some soil-borne fungal diseases such as *Pythium* and *Phytophthora*. Has systemic, residual properties. Can be used as drench for seed trays or dusted directly onto seeds.	
Malathion (Maldison)	General broad-spectrum insect control.	One of the oldest and most widely used insecticides.
Sodium Hypochlorite	Dipping cuttings, washing tools, benches and floors; kills most pests and diseases.	Can bleach clothing, can burn cuttings if too strong, dilute to use.

Chemical   Use

Thiram/Ziram Broad spectrum,
              non-systemic
              fungicides.
              Sometimes used as
              seed treatments, or
              for general
              protection.

Chemical control in greenhouses

Applying chemicals in greenhouses presents special problems. In normal greenhouse operations employees must work inside. Space is often limited and personal contact with plants and other treated surfaces is almost a certainty. Ventilation is often kept to a minimum to help maintain temperatures, but as a result mists, vapours and dusts may remain in the air for considerable periods.

Certain precautions should be followed to avoid problems when spraying in greenhouses:
• Use full safety equipment including respirators or gas masks, and full waterproof clothing.

• Put up warning signs on the outside of the greenhouse at all entrances.
• Do not enter the building without a face mask unless it has been fully aired for the length of time recommended on the chemical container label.
• All possible skin contact with treated plants should be avoided by workers and others, to minimise absorption of dangerous chemicals or skin irritants.
• Spray at a time of the week when it will be possible to avoid entering the greenhouse (largely) for a day or two after the spraying.

Forced convection, low volume sprayers

These are spray machines which disperse chemical solutions into smaller droplets, and in doing so, reduce the total quantity of chemical which needs to be used. Advantages are that chemical and labour costs can be reduced, the environment is less likely to be polluted, and the person operating the spray unit is less likely to be affected. However, the incidence of spray drift is increased because the

Soil sterilisation. Covers are pinned down over the soil, then steam or chemical is pumped underneath to kill pest and disease organisms in the soil.

Soil sterilisation trolley. The side wings can be folded up to enclose the potting mix during sterilisation, then folded down to make benches to work at when potting. When folded up, steam is pumped into the unit through a hose connected to the front.

droplets are smaller. As such these units are fine to use in confined spaces such as a greenhouse, but might not be as appropriate in open spaces.

Soil Fumigation to Control Diseases and Weeds

One method of controlling soil-borne organisms and pathogens is the use of fumigation. It is used for sterilising potting mixes, propagating mixes, and soil beds which are to be planted up in greenhouses.

Soil fumigation is a method of applying a poisonous chemical to a soil, allowing it to penetrate the soil as a vapour, and holding it in that condition for a period of time in order to eradicate unwanted organisms in the soil. Following this process the chemical will either break down in the soil into non or less toxic by-products, or is released from the soil so that planting can be carried out. Different types of fumigants control different types of problems.

In large areas fumigants can be applied by tractor-mounted injection equipment fitted to a rigid tine bar on the back of the tractor. In smaller areas a plastic sheet may be used to cover the soil and the fumigant is released under the sheet manually. Some types of fumigants (e.g. methyl bromide) which vaporise very quickly must be covered with a plastic sheet for a few days to prevent the chemical being lost. Other types of fumigants may be kept in the soil for the required period by simply rolling, watering or dragging the soil.

Contractors may be used to apply fumigants, or you can apply it yourself (provided the proper safety precautions are followed).

What is controlled?

Nematodes; soil-borne diseases such as *Verticillium*, *Phytophthora* and *Fusarium*; soil-dwelling insects; and most types of weed seeds and plants will be killed by fumigation. Some of the persistent weeds, such as kikuyu, nut grass and oxalis, may not be entirely eradicated, and depending on the chemical used, you may not get any control at all.

Examples Of Fumigants

The use of a particular fumigant will depend mainly upon the pests to be controlled. Some of the popular fumigants include:

• Bromafume

66% Methyl Bromide, 33% Chloropicrin — controls weeds, weed seeds, water moulds, nematodes, wireworms and many other soil pests.

• Vertafume

50% Methyl Bromide, 50% Chloropicrin — controls same problems as Bromafume plus *Verticillium, Fusarium*, damping off and *Botrytis*.

• Fungafume

33% Methyl Bromide, 66% Chloropicrin — controls same problems as Vertafume but not recommended for weed control other than grasses.

• Methyl Bromide

98% Methyl Bromide, 2% colouring agent — controls same problems as Bromafume.

• Edafume 60

60% Ethylene Dibromide — controls nematodes and other soil pests.

Note: Methyl bromide is now restricted or banned in some parts of the world.

Nursery Weed Control

Weed control in a nursery is very important for the following reasons:

• To remove plants that will compete for space, water and/or nutrients with your nursery stock.

• To remove plants that may act as hosts or attractants to pests and diseases.

• To remove plants that may be hazardous in some way to staff and customers (e.g. causing allergies, or having thorns or poisonous parts).

• To reduce the risk of fire.

• To create a tidy appearance.

Non-chemical Control

Common non-chemical control methods for use in nurseries include:

Hand weeding   Hand weeding is time-consuming but is useful for small infestations, or when there is major concern about the likelihood of spray damage to plants.

Mowing/slashing   Mowers, slashers and brush-cutters are very effective means of reducing unwanted plant growth. This method is good for large areas, particularly if you don't need to totally kill off the unwanted plants, and for those concerned about using chemical means.

Sterilisation   Steam sterilisation, or pasteurisation of growing and propagation media, will kill most pest and diseases, and most weed seeds. This results in fewer weeds germinating into growing areas or containers, making subsequent control programs much easier.

Solarisation   In this method clear plastic is spread over the soil, and the edges tucked into the soil or held down by heavy objects. High temperatures created beneath the plastic by sunlight energy will kill existing weeds, and encourage the germination and subsequent death of weed seeds in the soil.

Some weedicides for use at nurseries

Note 1: The following list of weedicides is not comprehensive, but contains some of the more widely used ones. The availability and particular use of these and other weedicides will vary from place to place, and is dependant on government regulations.

Note 2: When using a new chemical, or one that you are not familiar with, or if you are using it in a new situation, it is worthwhile doing a trial application first on a small section of the area. This allows you to gauge results before a full-scale application is carried out.

Control of weeds in nursery container stock

Oxadiazon (e.g. Ronstar)   Apply at time of potting then every 10 to 12 weeks throughout the year. Granular form is best. Product information sheets should be obtained, which list species that may be damaged or retarded by this chemical (some damage has been found to occur on *Hydrangea, Azalea, Erica, Cotoneaster, Berberis, Forsythia, Vinca,* Liliaceae plants, palms and *Spirea*). Ronstar 2G in granular form has been used widely for container weed control in the USA. Uniform application is essential (use an applicator if necessary).

Alternatives: DCPA (e.g. Dacthal) or Dichlobenil (e.g. Casoron). With all of these, contact with plant foliage should be avoided.

General knockdown weed control in outdoor areas

Tryquat   For most grasses and non-woody broadleaved weeds. Apply when weeds along paths, roads, fencelines, etc are becoming a problem. Do

not let weeds get to seeding stage before application.
Glyphosate (e.g. Roundup) For harder to kill
weeds. This chemical is more expensive than
Tryquat. Spray shields may be necessary to stop drift
onto nursery stock.

Control of woody shrubs and blackberries

Triclopyr (e.g. Garlon) is used for systemic control
of woody plants and broad-leaved weeds. It can be
sprayed or injected.

Control of weeds in enclosed areas, such as greenhouses and shadehouses

Dichlobenil (e.g. Casoron), Oxyfluorfen (e.g. Goal),
or Oxadiazon (e.g. Ronstar) applied when necessary.
Simazine may be used for pretreatment prior to
bringing plants into this type of area.

Control of established weeds in nursery stock

Fluazifop-Butyl (e.g. Fusilade) can be very effective
in controlling many established annual and
perennial grasses in nursery stock, without affecting
most broadleaved plants (shrubs and trees). Lists of
plants to avoid spraying with Fusilade can be
obtained from the manufacturer. This is most
effective sprayed when weeds are actively growing.

Controlling liverworts and mosses

Sprinkling a layer of coarse sand over the surface
of a pot will keep the surface dry and reduce these
problems. Alternatively, control with iron sulphate
sprays or drenches. In the UK Daconil Flowable 500
with Diphenamaid (Enide 50W) is applied every six
weeks to prevent this problem. Another method is
to spray 50% vinegar.

Example of a spray program in a propagation nursery in a warm, humid climate

There are basically five stages at which disease
control should be implemented:
1. Establishment and maintenance of stock plants
2. Collection of cuttings
3. Cutting preparation facility
4. Cutting preparation and striking techniques and
methods
5. Aftercare facility and care of cuttings
At different stages, different approaches may have
to be taken.

Propagation spray program:
Drench cuttings in Fongarid when still on bench.

Week 1 Benlate (0.5-1 g/L) + Aliette (1 g/L
drench);
or Terrazole (as directed);
or Terraclor (1 g/L);
or Thiram (1.5 g/L);
or Copper (2 g/L) + Mancozeb (2 g/L)
(for soft plants) + Oxychloride (as
directed)
Week 2 Rovral (1 g/L);
or Sportak (as directed);
or Topsin M (as directed)
Week 3 Bravo (1 g/L)
Fosject/Previcur (1 ml/L
drench)/Fongarid (1 g/L drench) may be
given as well
Mancozeb + Benlate for spot spraying
Week 5 Start with Terrazole or Terraclor if not
used previously
Week 7 Use Sportak or Topsin M or spot spray

Rules for Using Chemicals

1. *Only* use chemicals when actually needed!
2. Use the correct chemical for the job at hand; if
unsure, seek advice.
3. Always read the label, and the product
information sheets (if available).
4. Use protective clothing at all times.
5. Use the correct pesticide application equipment.
6. Don't spray on windy or very hot days!
7. Warn other people in the area that you are going
to spray (and have sprayed).
8. Wash out all spray equipment thoroughly when
finished.
9. Do not eat or smoke while spraying.
10. Wash all protective clothing thoroughly after
spraying.
11. Wash yourself thoroughly after spraying —
especially the hands.
12. Store spray equipment and chemicals in a safe,
locked place.
13. Dispose of empty pesticide containers according
to the label instructions.
14. Record all details of your spraying.

Keeping Records

Records of chemical usage are very important, particularly when using weedicides. The record will help nursery staff:

• improve pest control practices and avoid unnecessary chemical use;
• compare applications made with results achieved;
• purchase only the amounts of chemicals needed;
• reduce inventory carry over;
• establish proof that recommended procedures were followed if indemnity payments are involved.

What information should be kept:

• Varieties of plants treated
• Pests and weeds treated
• Location and size of area being treated
• Time of day, date and year
• Type of equipment used
• Pesticide used including name, type of formulation, trade name, manufacturer and batch number
• Amount used per hectare or per 100 litres of water
• Amount of active constituent (i.e. chemical) per hectare or per 100 litres water
• Stage of plant development (size of pot and size of plant)
• Pest/weed situation (e.g. severe, mild, etc)
• Weather, including temperature, wind, rainfall, etc.
• Whether the chemical was watered in afterwards
• Results of application; how long before pests/weeds died, how well it worked

Holding Stock

Sometimes plants reach a saleable size before the market is ready to buy them. In these instances, the nurseryperson is faced with the problem of keeping the plants alive and in peak condition without the plants growing further or becoming unmanageable. There are a variety of things which can be done including:

• slowing the growth rate by reducing fertiliser and water applications;
• potting up and selling as a larger plant;
• pruning and allowing regrowth to occur;
• dividing suckering or creeping plants;

• developing the plant into a different product, e.g. turning it into a bonsai, topiary, basket or tub specimen.

Holding dormant plants

Some plants, in particular bulbs, deciduous plants and many herbaceous perennials, go through a period of dormancy (usually over winter), when growth slows considerably, or stops. During this time, the plants are easy to move, and for that reason they are often sold as balled plants or bare-rooted (without any soil).

Bare-rooted plants and bulbs are much easier and cheaper to transport and store in a dormant state, hence the costs involved in marketing are reduced. However, it is essential to understand the requirements of dormant or semi-dormant plants. When growth slows, the plants' ability to resist pest and disease problems can also be reduced. The plants will only remain dormant as long as environmental conditions are appropriate, and placing them in a warmer situation might stimulate growth and make the plants susceptible to damage through drying out or physical damage when moved. They need to be sold, potted or planted out before dormancy breaks and growth resumes.

Bare-rooted plants should be stored with their roots covered by a moist (but not saturated) material such as wood shavings or they can be heeled into a bed of soil. They can be bunched together and do not need to be stood up, but be careful that plants rubbing against each other do not cause too many wounds.

Some varieties of herbaceous perennials, bulbs, corms, rhizomes and tubers can be stored dry on shelves in a dark, cool place over winter; while others must be kept moist, perhaps in containers covered with moist moss or shavings.

Nurseries which grow plants that go through a period of dormancy may need to build special storage facilities to hold plants for several months after digging as orders are received and processed.

Plant Modification

Shape, height, flowering and other characteristics of a plant are affected by many different things, including the environment and the way in which the plant is treated in the nursery. It is always preferable to grow plants that are uniform in appearance. Plants of a particular variety generally look and sell better when all plants are the same height, width and colour. Producing uniform batches of plants is an increasingly important aspect of nursery management.

Plant modification techniques are being more widely used to give desired characteristics. Some of the techniques used are outlined below:

Developing a thicker or sturdier stem or trunk

Moisture: Trickle-irrigated trees develop a greater trunk diameter than non-irrigated trees. A lack of moisture slows growth and causes stems to become thicker and sturdier.

Light: Adequate light is important to producing thicker and sturdier stems. Placing plants in full sun or under artificial lights will promote stem development.

Spacing: If there is plenty of space between plants, they do not need to grow upwards to compete for light, hence stems become thicker.

Fertilising: Reduce nitrogen to reduce lush vegetative growth.

Pruning: Cutting a plant back makes the trunk thicken, but it can also extend the time taken to get a saleable plant.

Wind: Wind makes photosynthesates move towards the bottom of a plant rather than the top.

Applications: Used for deciduous trees where a sturdy, thick stem is important; for bonsai; and in warm climates or greenhouses where plants grow too fast and the stem can become too weak to support the lush, heavy top growth. Growing-on nurseries prefer to buy plants with a thicker and sturdier stem, because this, more than height, will affect the performance when they are grown on.

Making a plant taller

Light: In restricted light, plants grow taller to reach the light above, therefore shade can be used to promote taller growth.

Moisture: Frequent watering promotes taller growth.

Fertilising: Liquid nitrogenous fertilisers applied frequently usually promote taller growth than slow release fertilisers.

Spacing: Plants spaced close together compete for light and grow taller.

Day length: In many plants day length affects the formation of flower buds. By varying day length (e.g. having a period when lights switch on at night, or using lights to extend the length of day), the plants can be kept in vegetative growth, in turn encouraging a bigger plant.

Pruning: Remove side shoots to encourage terminal growth; staking can also encourage more growth at the top of the plant.

Chemicals: In some woody plants gibberellic acid will encourage growth.

Applications: Trees, rootstocks for standards.

Developing a compact root system

Fertiliser: Applying fertiliser to soil near the base of the plant will encourage root growth to remain close to the base.

Drip irrigation: This can keep the zone close to the base of the tree moist when the surrounding soil is dry, hence roots do not spread in search of water.

Root pruning: Plants grown in the open ground can be pruned regularly with a 'U' or 'L' shaped tractor-mounted blade which cuts through the soil. Plants in containers are sometimes root pruned to remove old or diseased roots and encourage healthier, more vigorous root growth.

Cultivation: By rotary hoeing between nursery rows, weeds can be controlled and roots cut, encouraging root growth to stay closer to the base of the plant.

Copper screening: A copper screen is buried below the soil where root growth is to stop. Roots will not grow through the copper.

Root control bags: Made from a special fabric, these bags are buried below the ground with plants planted into them. Water flows through the fabric easily, so drainage is not a problem.

Containers: Pots which absorb heat (e.g. metal and high density plastics) discourage root growth close to the sides of the container. Pots which have better insulation properties (e.g. paper fibre or wood) encourage growth close to the sides of the container.

Applications: Trees and advanced plants grown in the open ground.

Encouraging compact, bushy growth

Pruning: Removing terminal growth forces more side shoots. Lack of staking encourages more lower growth.

Environment: Exposing a plant to harsher or more

exposed conditions (e.g. wind) generally encourages denser and lower growth.

Chemicals: Some hormones reduce the internodal space (i.e. the gap between leaves on the stem).

Light: Adequate light is essential for compact growth. Avoid shading.

Spacing: Allow more space between plants to reduce competition for light.

Moisture: Less generous watering can make some plants grow more compact.

Applications: To produce plants with greater stability and more attractive appearance, including indoor plants or potted colour.

Improving foliage colour and vigour

Light: Different plants react differently to light. Many shade-loving plants will develop burnt, or at least poorer coloured foliage in full sun. Other plants (e. g. coleus, croton) can lose the brilliance of foliage colour in inadequate light.

Moisture: Frequent watering and perfect drainage will promote better growing conditions and generally encourage more luxuriant growth. Poor drainage can reduce chlorophyll and make leaves less green.

Feeding: Different nutrients can affect quantity and colour of foliage in different plants. Ample nitrogen usually promotes leaf growth.

Applications: A wide range of plants including bedding plants, indoor plants, shade loving plants and many general lines.

Encouraging flower development

Plant maturity: Cutting-grown plants often flower earlier if cuttings are taken from mature stock plants.

Day length: Using artificial lighting and shading can be used to stimulate (or stop) flowering, and control plant growth so that flowers are produced at the time the plant is to be marketed.

Chemicals: Some chemical hormone sprays can encourage flowering, but many of these techniques are still experimental.

Ringbarking: Partial or complete ringbarking of a stem (i.e. girdling) puts stress on a plant which stimulates flowering in some species. On the wrong type of plant this can cause death.

Carbon-nitrogen ratio in propagation mix: Flowering is usually encouraged by a higher carbon/nitrogen ratio.

Pruning: If done at the right time of year, root pruning can stress some plants and stimulate flowering. By understanding what type of wood the flowers occur on, the nurseryperson can adapt pruning practices to either retain or stimulate the appropriate type of growth for flowering.

Applications: Plants in flower sell better and are preferred by retailers.

Chemical Growth Modification

Various chemicals have different types of effects on the growth habits of different plants. A few of the many chemical modifiers include:

- Gibberellic acid accelerates the growth in some woody plants.
- Succinic acid, Maleichydrazide, abscissic acid and ancymidol inhibits the growth of some plants.
- Naphthalene Acetic Acid (NAA) can inhibit sprouting of buds after pruning on some plants.

Getting plants to flower out of season

Flowering occurs when there is a sudden change in the growing point from vegetative organs (i.e. leaves, stems and leaf buds) to floral organs. When this happens, the apical dominance usually weakens. The initial stimulus to cause this change in tissue type appears to normally (but not always) originate in the leaves.

As flowering tends to be related to particular times of the year, the initial stimulus is most obviously environmental. There are three possible types of environmental stimuli:

1. Physical, e.g. changes in atmospheric pressure
2. Electrical, e.g. changes in pH
3. Chemical (changes in levels of certain chemicals), e.g. light increases photosynthesis, which increases levels of sugar

Types of Flowering Responses

Temperature can affect time of flowering from sowing in three different ways:

1. Vernalisation — the process whereby cold temperature hastens flowering.
2. Rate of flowering process increases over a sequence of different temperatures. The final stage is an optimum temperature where flowering is most rapid.

3. Supra optimal temperatures — stressful temperatures which delay flowering as temperatures become warmer.

Examples of Flowering Control

Narcissus

Flower formation begins in the bulb during late spring and is completed by late summer or early autumn. The stage of flower development is important, as the bulbs give their best response to cool treatments once the trumpet has formed. In their natural habitat in Southern Europe and the Mediterranean, their growth cycle is as follows:

Hot dry summer — in early summer, old leaves and flowers die, new leaves and flowers are initiated; in mid to late summer, leaf and flower formation completed.

Warm autumn — new root growth begins, and shoot starts but does not emerge.

Cool wet winter — leaves emerge through soil, flower elongates within leaves.

Warm spring — rapid growth of leaves and flowering.

Forcing Schedule

1. Harvest bulbs in summer.
2. Store at 17°C until flower bud development is completed. This normally takes 2–4 weeks. Temperatures should not go above 20°C, otherwise flowering will be delayed.
3. Cooling treatment before and after boxing: hold the bulbs at 9°C treatment for 6 weeks to promote early flowering. If you want late flowering, hold at the bulbs at 17°C.
4. Plant bulbs in boxes of peat or straw. The earlier the plants are boxed, the earlier they flower.
5. Place boxes in forcing house. This is done when flower bud is at the neck of the bulb (later for late flowering, earlier for early flowering).
6. Grow on in house, until flowering. A temperature of 15°C is used when forcing.

Forcing with lights

Place boxes under clear or pearl tungsten lights (60 or 100W) 1–1.5 metres above the crop on a 1.1 metre grid spacing. Give 7 hours lighting every 24 hours.

High temperature

For early flowering bulbs, hold the bulbs at 35°C for 5 days immediately after lifting in late spring. This treatment will not work once the warm weather in summer commences.

Azaleas

Azaleas respond to vernalisation, i.e. flowering is hastened by cool temperatures. Plants with well developed flower buds are stored at 10°C or less. Keep the plants at 2°C (no lower) for extended storage, or 9–10°C for short storage periods.

There has been some evidence that shows short photoperiods (i.e. short hours of daylight) promotes flowering, although there is some controversy over these findings.

Growing plants are pinched to promote bushiness. After pinching the plants are kept at 18°C for 6 weeks on long photoperiods, followed by 18°C with short photoperiods. The plants are then placed in cold storage at 7°C for 6 weeks, followed by a further 3–6 weeks growth at 16–18°C.

Light and plant growth

Light is essential for plant growth — for vegetative growth, flowers and fruit. Provided the plant receives the correct amount and quality of light, the plant will continue to thrive.

The light spectrum can be separated into its colours, all of which affect plants differently. For example, the blue spectrum is involved in phototropic responses (the bending of plants towards the light source), while green light actually has little effect on plant growth.

The intensity and duration of the light source is important. Some plants, known as short-day plants, flower when the days become shorter, others are known as long-day plants. However, this is not the rule as some plants flower irrespective of light duration and are known as day-neutral plants. These flowering responses are controlled by the red/far-red phytochrome pigments of light.

Greenhouse structures frequently use artificial lighting to assist plant growth. Plants respond in different ways because different lamps radiate different qualities of the light spectrum.

Lamp	Stem Elongation	Bushiness	Flowering	Other Effects
Fluorescent	yes—slowly	yes	long period	horizontal leaf
Plant lamps (Gro-Lux)	yes—slowly	yes	late	deep green leaf
Wide spectrum (Gro-Lux WS, Vita-lite, Agro-lite)	yes—quickly	no	quickens	light green leaf; plants age fast
High intensity discharge (Deluxe mercury or metal halide)	yes—slowly	yes	long period	green leaf expands; similar to fluorescent
High-pressure sodium	yes—slowly	yes	late	green leaf expands; extra thick stems
Low-pressure sodium	yes—slowly	yes	yes	deep green leaf; leaf expands; very thick stems
Incandescent leaf	yes—excessive becoming spindly	no	rapidly	pale thin elongated leaf; plants age fast

Pots placed on raised mesh platforms over concrete assist drainage and hygiene. The only disadvantage is that the plants are exposed to the drying effect of wind.

Wrapping plants in tissue paper or cellophane improves presentation and increases the plants' gift potential.

Trolleys are used to move plants about and to provide mobile displays in retail nurseries.

Some plants lend themselves to being clipped into different shapes. These plants may be grown with the specific intention of creating a topiary; alternatively topiary may be developed from old stock which has grown too large to sell as a 'normal' plant.

Herb starter kits. Plant kits are sometimes sold as novelty items in retail nurseries. Supplementary material such as containers, fertiliser or information sheets can also be added to the kits.

This impatiens is at an ideal stage to sell to the retailer. The large number of flower buds means that it will continue flowering (and hence attract customers' attention) for some time.

Growing several varieties of plants in one large container, such as this cacti garden, can increase the plants' marketability. The same concept has been used effectively with other plant groups including perennials and herbs.

Good signs create a positive image and help to sell plants. (Deborah Law's Fuchsia Farm, Mt Tamborine, Queensland)

5 Nursery Materials

The choice of materials can have a major impact on the productivity and profitability of a nursery. Without good quality materials you will not grow attractive, saleable plants.

Potting Mixes

Container plants are grown in a variety of different media. Some are mainly a mixture of soils, others are mixtures which include no soil at all. Some potting media are combinations of soil and non-soil components.

The ideal potting medium should have the following characteristics:
- The mix should be free of weed seeds and pest or disease organisms.
- It should be freely draining and with good aeration (see chapter 3).
- It should be able to retain sufficient nutrients and moisture for healthy plant growth.
- Waste salts from fertilisers should leach out of the soil easily.
- The mix should be heavy enough to make the pot stable, but light enough to minimise the effort involved in lifting the pots.
- The mix should be of consistent quality throughout.

To make quality potting mix with uniform characteristics requires components which are of a very even quality (i.e. not much variation in particle size or chemical properties), and to acheive this usually requires very expensive screening and mixing equipment. This means that high quality potting mixes are generally produced by specialist companies.

In many parts of the world, potting mix companies still operate with less sophisticated equipment and produce variable mixes. Because good potting mix equipment is very expensive, the best mixes are also expensive. In Australia high quality potting mixes can now be purchased carrying the Australian Standards Logo (see page 51).

Potting media may utilise a combination of any number of different media. The availability and cost of components can vary greatly from place to place, so the components which are readily available are normally those which are used. Nurseries in isolated areas may have to make their own mixes, but in more populated areas there are usually several large and reputable companies offering a wide variety of mixes.

Nurseries which grow a wide variety of plants may need to use a variety of mixes, but nurseries growing one type of plant may be able to use just one or two types of mixes.

Soil-based Potting Mixes

John Innes Potting Mixes
In the late 1930s the John Innes Research Institute in the UK began developing a series of loam based

composts. They were popular for many years, although the scarcity of quality components and the need to sterilise the mix has meant that many nursery growers now prefer standardised soilless mixes.

Seed compost

2 parts loam (pH 6.3), 1 part sand, 1 part peat plus 1.2 kg superphosphate and 0.58 kg ground limestone/cubic metre

Potting compost

7 parts loam, 3 parts peat, 2 parts sand plus 2.9 kg superphosphate and 0.58 kg limestone/cubic metre.

Other soil-based potting mixes that may be worth trying include the following:
1. Heavy soils, such as clay loams: 1 part soil, 2 parts perlite or sand, 2 parts peat moss
2. Medium soils, such as silt loams: 1 part soil, 1 part perlite or sand, 1 part peat moss
3. Light soils, such as sandy loams: 1 part soil, 1 part peat moss

For each 35 litres of the above mixes add:
224 g dolomitic limestone (provides calcium and magnesium). For acid loving plants use calcium sulphate as a substitute.
280g superphosphate (20%) (provides phosphorus and sulphur)

Source: Hartmann, et al, 1990, *Plant Propagation* (5th Ed).

Soilless mixes

In recent years soilless mixes have become popular, largely due to the unreliability of soil components in mixes. Many of the soilless mixes are based upon pine bark chips. However, bark and other timber components have a disadvantage in that they are contaminated with toxic chemicals when fresh. Proper composting before mixing can overcome this problem however some soil companies have been known to supply mixes which are still contaminated.

During the 1980s the Knoxfield Research Station in Victoria conducted research programs on potting mixes. A recommended mix for short-term (about 6-12 months) container plants is 8 parts pinebark, 3 parts coarse washed river sand and 1 part brown coal (lignite).

Two fertiliser strategies for use with this mix are:
1. 1.0 kg Osmocote 3-4 month (15-5.2-12)
   2.0 kg Osmocote 8-9 month (18-4.3-8.3)
   0.5 kg GU 49 or Osmocote coated iron
   0.5 kg Micromax
   Dolomite to bring pH between 5.5 and 6.0 (2 kg)
2. 1.0kg IBDU
   3.0 kg Osmocote 8-9month (18-4.3-8.3)
   0.5 kg GU 49 or Osmocote coated iron
   0.5 kg Micromax
   Dolomite to bring the pH to between 5.5 and 6.0 (2 kg)

Note: amounts of fertiliser given are for one cubic metre of mix.

U.C. Potting Mixes

The University of California began to develop a series of mixes in 1941. The *U.C. System for Producing Healthy Container Grown Plants,* published in 1957, outlines not only these mixes but also many other basic practices used in the modern nursery. These mixes are based on a mixture of peat and fine sand.

The Five Main U.C. Mixes

Mix	Fine sand %	Peat %	Comments
A	100	0	Seldom used heavy mix; used in beds or trays.
B	75	25	Commonly used; good physical properties; used in containers, trays or beds.
C	50	50	Frequently used; excellent physical properties; used in containers.
D	25	75	Light mix; excellent aeration; used in pots.
E	0	100	Very light weight; used for azaleas, camellias and gardenias, etc.

Fertilisers and often lime are added to the U.C. mixes to provide nutrients and to adjust the pH to the appropriate level.

The Cornell Peat-Lite Mixes

These mixes produce a lightweight, uniform, soilless

medium suitable for plant growth. The mixes do not require sterilisation.

Peat-Lite Mix A

To make 0.76 m³ (1 cubic yard):
  0.39 m³ shredded sphagnum peat moss
  0.39 m³ horticultural grade vermiculite
  2.25 kg grounded dolomite limestone
  0.45-0.9 kg single superphosphate (20%), preferably powdered
  0.45kg calcium nitrate
  84 g fritted trace elements
  56 g iron sequestrene (330)
  84 g wetting agent

Peat-Lite Mix B

The mix is the same as Mix A, except that horticultural perlite is substituted for vermiculite.

Peat-Lite Mix C

This mix is used for germinating seeds
  0.035 m³ shredded sphagnum peat moss
  0.035 m³ No. 4 horticultural vermiculite
  42 g ammonium nitrate
  42 g superphosphate (20%), powdered
  210 g ground dolomite limestone

The addition of slow release fertilisers is beneficial for plants which will remain in the mix for extended periods.

In 1984 Kevin Handreck and Neil Black published an excellent reference book, *Growing Media for Ornamental Plants & Turf*, published by NSW University Press. This is a comprehensive and practical book and is probably one of the most useful references for the nursery worker.

Australian Standards for Potting Mixes

Australian Standards have recently been established for packaged potting mixes (No. 3743-1989). All mixes bearing the Australian Standards Mark are subjected to regular testing, both at the manufacturing plant and by independent laboratories under the supervision of Standards Australia.

There are two Australian Standard potting mix grades: Regular and Premium. Both mixes must be freely draining, while capable of holding a good supply of water. Both must be easy to rewet if they

dry out, they must be free of toxins and have a pH in the range 5.3-6.5.

Both mixes should contain a full range of trace elements in sufficient quantities to last for at least one year of plant growth, as well as ample amounts of phosphorus, calcium, magnesium and sulphur.

Regular mixes are not required to contain soluble nitrogen. Premium mixes must contain soluble nitrogen and be able to continue providing enough soluble nitrogen for at least one month of plant growth. Premium mixes generally contain slow release fertiliser and will have been made from high quality materials such as composted pine bark and peat.

Some potting mixes state that they conform to Australian Standards, but do not carry the Standards Mark. These products have not been tested by Standards Australia so there is no guarantee of the quality of the mix. The names of potting mixes that have been approved to carry the Standards Mark can be obtained by ringing Standards Australia (Ph: 02 963 4111).

Components of Potting Mixes

Soils
• Soils have a good buffering capacity so pH changes are slow to take place.
• Soils do not have the complicated chemical toxicity problems which can occur in soilless mixes. For this reason, it can be beneficial to include some soil in 'soilless' mixes.
• Many pests and diseases are soil-borne so soilless mixes generally have fewer of these problems.
• Reliable supplies with 'known' characteristics are difficult to obtain.

Sand
The ideal sand for potting mixes is a coarse granitic sand. This is the same type of sand used in fish aquariums. Calcareous sands are very alkaline and unsuited to plant growth. Beach sand is not suitable because of its high levels of salt.

Some sands contain a lot of dust or other fine material when purchased and these need to be washed out before it is used. Sand is often mixed with other water retaining materials, such as peat or vermiculite, to obtain a balanced media.
• Supply of sands with 'known' characteristics is more reliable than many other components.

- Sands can be added to mixes to improve drainage and aeration.
- Sand makes pots heavier to move.
- Sand is virtually inert, i.e. it has no effect on the chemical balance of the mix.

Peat

- Peat moss is lightweight, porous, well aerated and drains well.
- It mixes well with other components, but often requires thorough moistening before use (if it dries out it can be difficult to wet).
- The pH can be low (i.e. 4 or 4.5) and mixes incorporating peat may need lime added to offset this effect.
- Occasionally some types of peat can be found with a salt toxicity.
- There is growing concern over the use of peat because it takes many years to form and available sources are dwindling rapidly.
- High quality peat can be expensive.

Pine bark

Shredded pine bark is available in a range of grades (i.e. different sized lumps). Fresh pine bark is toxic to plants and must be composted for several months before use.

- Bark which has not been composted ties up nitrogen available to the plant. Plants grown in mixes with fresh bark may show symptoms of nitrogen deficiency (i.e. yellowing of the older leaves).
- Bark which has a resinous smell or is reddish in colour should be composted before use.
- It is frequently used in proportions of 50-70% of the potting mixture.

Sawdust

Like pine bark, sawdust has problems with toxins and nitrogen availability. Hardwood sawdust should be composted for six weeks or more, adding the following fertiliser to every cubic metre of sawdust being composted:

> 2.6 kg urea
> 2.0 kg superphosphate (less if growing phosphorus-sensitive plants)
> 0.5 kg potassium sulphate
> 18 kg dolomite (for a final pH of 6.5)
> 9 kg dolomite (for a final pH of 6.0)
> 5 kg dolomite (for a final pH of 5.5)

Trace elements can also be added in small quantities.

Lignite

Also called lignapeat or brown coal, this substance is not coal, but is taken from coal mines. It has a very good waterholding capacity, which can be a problem in keeping the mix too wet if used in large quantities. It can be very dusty, and will stain clothing and hands. The main advantage is its cheap cost.

Coal ash

Coal ash is taken out of industrial furnaces and burners after the burning of black coal (brown coal ash is not suitable). After cooling with water, the ash is taken from the furnace, then crushed and sieved.

- Ash sieved between a 3/16 to 1/4 inch sieve has given excellent results as a propagating medium.
- Ash can develop compaction problems over time. As such it is often unsuitable for potting mixes.
- Nutrient content, pH and other properties can vary from source to source, affecting its suitability for growing plants.
- In coastal areas ash is sometimes cooled with salt water, leaving it contaminated and unsuitable for growing plants.

Vermiculite

This is a mineral derived from mica mined in South Africa and the USA. The mineral is treated in a number of ways including heating at temperatures of nearly 1079°C (2000°F) to obtain the product used in horticulture.

Vermiculite is very light and spongy in appearance. It retains air, water and nutrients very well. The pH of vermiculite is sometimes slightly acid or slightly alkaline, although rarely enough to pose much of a problem with growth.

Vermiculite needs to be mixed with other media to get the best results. Even though it retains air well, it can retain too much water for many plants. If used on its own it can after a year or so turn puggy (i.e. the structure can collapse). However, mixed with gravel or sand (no more than 40 or 50% vermiculite) it retains its structure, and drainage is improved.

Perlite

Like vermiculite, perlite is a processed mineral. It has excellent waterholding properties but is less spongy and better drained than vermiculite. Perlite is often used by itself for propagation or in a 50/50 mixture with vermiculite. (This type of mix can become too wet in some situations, though). Perlite can have a neutral or slightly acid pH.

The source of perlite is important as the quality of perlite varies. Some Australian perlite contains too much fine material. Sieved or graded perlite is generally preferred. Being predominantly white, growth of algae can be a problem. It can be expensive. Like vermiculite it is relatively light weight.

Expanded plastics

These materials are inert, and in many cases, relatively inexpensive. Their major disadvantages are:

• they do not retain moisture or nutrients very well;
• they are very light weight and when mixed with other materials often separate and float to the top.

After a couple of months, what was originally a mix can end up as a layer of the expanded plastic on top of the rest of the media.

Examples include polystyrene (bean bag) balls, hygropor (a mix of ureaformaldehyde and polystyrol), and polystryrol.

Scoria

Scoria is a porous volcanic rock which can be obtained in a wide variety of grades. The physical properties of scoria are excellent, but its pH can vary greatly according to where it comes from (the pH ranges from 7 to 10). Scoria which has a high pH needs to be kept moist and left outdoors for up to 12 months to remove excess lime before it is used.

It can be abrasive on soft stems, so should be avoided for growing seedlings. The cost of scoria is usually dependent on the distance it has to be transported. If you are close to a scoria quarry it can be a cheap material to use in the potting mix. In Australia scoria is readily available in parts of Victoria and North Queensland.

Leca (expanded clay)

This material is made by blending and bloating clay in rotary kilns. The material looks like hard terracotta balls. It has a medium drainage and waterholding capacity. In some countries it can be very expensive. It is popular for use in water-well type pots for indoor plants.

Others

Other components which have been used include rice hulls, peanut shells, spent mushroom compost, sewage sludge and blue metal.

Water Repellence in Potting Mixes

Waxy layers on organic material repel water. This can make some soils repel water when they are dry. For example, a mix containing a lot of peat moss will usually absorb water when wet, but if it dries out, water may run off the surface and down the sides of the pot leaving the root ball dry.

Water repellence can be reduced by adding sand to the mix or applying wetting agents (i.e. synthetic surfactants). Wetting agents are similar to soaps and dishwashing liquids although you should be aware that dishwashing liquids are biodegradable and will not provide a lasting effect.

Many wetting agents on the market become useless after a short period. Research by Kevin Handreck at the CSIRO has indicated that the two most effective wetting agents in Australia are 'Wettasoil' and 'Aquasoil-Wetta'. After eight months both products were still effective.

Propagation Media

The material or combination of materials that you use as a propagation media should should have the following properties:

Physical properties

• The media should provide good physical support to the plants.
• The media should be reasonably light, easy to handle and easy to stick cuttings into. Sharp-edged materials, such as scoria, may be a problem with germinating seedlings.
• The materials used should not readily degrade or break down once in use.
• The media should have good aeration. This will aid water penetration and drainage, give adequate provision for the exchange of gases (i.e. root absorption of oxygen and release of CO_2), and provide space for roots to grow.

A mixture of particles ranging in size from around 1 mm to 5 mm, with the addition of very fine particles from materials such as peat or pine bark generally provides a suitable mix.

Once a medium is watered the volume of pore space containing air is reduced. The percentage of a medium filled with air when just drained is commonly called its air-filled porosity or air space. A propagation medium should have an air space of at least 27% evenly spread throughout its volume, although this figure will vary according to the plant you are cultivating. For example, cuttings of aerial rooting plants require a much higher available air space. The provision of misting will also generally require an increase in the air space of the medium. The upper limit should be no more than about 35–40%.

Determining Air Space

This can be simply done by lining a propagation tray or pot with thin plastic and filling the container with moist, but not wet, propagation medium. The medium is then watered until the water level reaches the surface of the medium. A hole is then cut in the bottom of the plastic so that excess water can drain away. This water should be collected and the volume measured. The volume is roughly equivalent to the volume of available air space for that media in that type of container. The percentage of air space can be calculated by:

$$\frac{\text{Volume of water}}{\text{Volume of media}} \times 100$$

Chemical properties

Propagation media should have the following chemical properties:
- It should be chemically stable during use.
- For most plants it should have a pH in the range of 4-6 (some will plants will grow better at a higher pH). The pH can be increased by the addition of lime and decreased by increasing the percentage of materials with low pH such as peat moss and pine bark.
- It should be low in salts and other harmful chemicals

Biological properties

The propagation media should be as free as possible of harmful organisms such as weed seeds, spores, and insects.

Mixes/substrates for striking cuttings and germinating seed

The commonly used mixes are as follows:

1. Sand and peat   Normally 75% coarse washed sand and 25% shredded peat moss. In some cases proportions can range from 100% peat for germinating fern spores to 90% sand for cuttings or seed under continuous mist systems.

2. Sand and perlite   Normally 50% sand and 50% perlite.

3. Peat and perlite   Normally 10% peat and 90% perlite. In some cases 100% perlite is used.

4. Vermiculite and sand   Normally 75% sand and 25% vermiculite (never more than 40% vermiculite).

5. Rockwool   A material made by spinning fibres of molten rock. Only use horticultural grades. It has a very good ability to hold both air and water (only 3% solids). Not widely used, but very promising.

6. Polystyrene and peat   Normally 50% polystyrene to 50% peat. Polystyrene must only be mixed with lightweight material such as peat.

Nutrition Management

Types of Fertilisers

Plants in pots have a very limited amount of nutrients available to them. While plants growing in the ground can send roots further afield to search out nutrients, plants grown in containers must be supplied with an adequate supply of nutrients as close to the trunk as possible. Nurseries use a variety of fertilisers including the following:

Uncoated pellets and tablets

These are fertilisers which are compressed or stuck together in a small pellet or tablet. Because it takes time for the tablet to break down, the release of nutrients is slowed and the plant is supplied with food over an extended period of time.

Coated pellets (e.g. Osmocote, Nutricote and Macrocote)

Similar to uncoated pellets, but with a covering of wax or some other material which slows down the dispersion of nutrients into the soil. Different types of coatings will react differently under varying weather and soil conditions, so the product used should be selected carefully according to where and when it is to be used.

Organic fertilisers

These are complex chemicals derived from organic sources, such as seaweeds, fishmeal and bone meal, which often need to undergo chemical changes in the soil before they release nutrients to a plant. These changes are gradual, so the supply of nutrients is spread over a period.

Inorganic powders and granules

These are simple chemicals which usually only need a small amount of water before the plant can absorb them. They are generally fast acting, but tend to leach through the soil rapidly. They are best applied in small amounts at frequent intervals during periods of rapid growth. Because they act so fast, they are also more likely to burn roots or foliage if applied heavily.

Liquid fertilisers

These are very fast acting and can be absorbed as soon as they make contact with the plant.

Applying Fertilisers

The main ways of providing nutrients to plants in a nursery are as follows:

1. *Mixing straight (organic or inorganic) fertilisers into the media before plants are potted up, and following with applications of liquid fertilisers at regular intervals*

Soil/media which has such fertiliser incorporated into it must be used quickly (within a week or two of adding the fertiliser). The fertiliser can leach out or change form if left for any period.

2. *Mixing fertilisers into the media before potting, then adding additional fertiliser by topdressing pots or ground at the base of the plants*

Frequency of topdressing will depend on the type of fertiliser being used and the characteristics of the potting mix or soil to leach out or retain nutrients.

3. *Mixing slow release fertilisers such as Osmocote into the media before plants are potted (or planted if in the open ground)*

It is important to note that slow release fertilisers might not feed the plant for its entire life in the nursery. Temperature and moisture can affect how quickly or slowly the fertiliser is depleted. Some fertilisers do not work at all in cooler climates during the winter months, and should normally be used only in subtropical or tropical regions.

Any fertiliser mixed into the medium must be mixed thoroughly and evenly. Some nurseries use a cement mixer; others have the soil supplier mix the fertiliser for them.

4. *Applying slow release fertiliser to the base of the plant after planting or potting*

This method is preferred by some because different types of fertilisers can be applied to different plants, and it does not have the problem of having to ensure a thorough mixing of fertiliser in the soil/potting mix.

It is important that the person doing this job does not over or underfeed — a pinch of slow release fertiliser is not enough! A set measure per plant is required to prevent variations in growth habits and rates.

5. *Using liquid fertilisers only, applied through sprays or the normal watering system (sometimes called fertigation)*

Liquid feeding can vary from daily applications to every once every five or six weeks. There are arguments for both ways. The danger is that overfeeding can burn plants and underfeeding will not achieve the growth required. The rate of feeding must be calculated carefully, and the application of liquid feeds should be very precise.

Applying Nutrients at the Propagation Stage

Nurserypersons tend to vary in their attitude towards using nutrients or fertilisers during the propagation stage. Some believe it enhances propagation, others see no overall benefit.

Research has shown some benefit with some plants, but there is no general consensus as to the benefits of widespread fertilising during propagation. In most cases, fertilisers are not readily absorbed by cuttings until roots begin to develop. Medium to high concentration of fertilisers may damage newly developing roots. Fertiliser applications may also encourage the development of other organisms such as algae, or encourage the foliage of cuttings to grow at the expense of root

development. However, some slow rooting cuttings may benefit from weak foliar applications.
• Nutrients added to the mist system during propagation have been shown to promote root and shoot growth in some woody plants.
• Generally nutrients are applied as soon as possible after roots appear on the cutting.
• The level of nutrient application for optimum growth varies between plant varieties. (This level has been shown to be the same for older plants as it is for young seedlings or rooted cuttings.)
• The balance between carbon and nitrogen has a significant effect on root formation. A high carbon or carbohydrate level and low to moderate nitrogen level favours rooting of dormant cuttings. (Without leaves, decidous hardwood cuttings must rely on stored carbohydrate because it isn't possible for photosynthesis to occur and produce new carbohydrate). High nitrogen tends to reduce rooting.
• By reducing feeding of nitrogen to stock plants before taking cuttings, the levels of nitrogen in the cutting material can be reduced, and this in turn can stimulate rooting when the cutting is taken.
• There is little evidence to suggest that adding nutrients helps root initiation, but there is evidence with some species that adding nutrients after root initiation will help speed root development.

Fertilising Problems

Mosses, algae and liverworts often grow on the surface of the media in pots. This can be indicative of dampness, but also can result from fertilisers lying on the surface of the media. A layer of coarse sand on the top of the pot will restrict light to the fertilised soil and hence deter the growth of mosses and liverworts.

A white cake on top of the medium indicates a build-up of salts from fertilisers. This can damage plants, and generally indicates overfeeding or insufficient leaching away of waste salts.

Runoff from a nursery (excess water flowing through the soil or pots) will usually contain higher levels of salts and unused fertilisers. These chemicals can eventually lead to soil and other pollution problems as they drain away from the nursery into neighbouring properties. Legislation has been introduced, or is being introduced in parts of Australia, America and other countries to force

nurseries to collect and treat 'polluted' water draining from the nursery. This could become a significant expense for nurseries in the future.

Hot, wet conditions can make some fertilisers release their nutrients too fast, burning the roots of plants, and/or wasting fertiliser.

Application of Liquid Fertilisers

The simplest device is a standard chemical sprayer. Because of the quantity of plants being fed, the fertiliser is normally applied in a concentrated solution and the plants are immediately watered to wash the fertiliser off the leaves and into the pots (preventing burning of the leaves).

A better method involves automatic mixing of the fertiliser into the irrigation system using an injection device such as a Geewa. These units are precise, and allow the fertiliser to be applied at very low concentrations, regularly, quickly and with very low labour costs.

Labels

There are two main types of labels used in a nursery. These are promotional labels which are used to sell the plant at the nursery, and plant labels which are attached to the plant or pot and taken home with the customer.

Plant labels fall into the following categories:

Category	Good points	Bad points
Solid plastic (stick in)	Strong; durable; inexpensive; reusable	Not attractive; sometimes lost under foliage; can be removed
Cardboard (tie on)	Cheap, easy to see	Can ringbark plant if left on too long; will decompose or be eaten by snails, etc.
Flexible plastic (stick in)	Medium cost; medium durability; water resistant	Become brittle; not reusable
Flexible plastic (tie on)	Medium cost; medium durability; can place in a prominent position on plant	Become brittle when exposed to sun; may eventually ringbark the plant

Another factor to be considered with labels is whether or not to use printed labels.

Printed (writing only)

Printed labels save the time and effort required for writing labels and they allow more information to be included on the label (i.e. plant description as well as the nursery name). They can be expensive if growing or selling a large variety of plants.

Printed (picture labels)

These contain a photograph of the plant on one side and a description on the reverse. They are a very good sales tool, and are especially good for selling plants when they are not at their most attractive (e.g. deciduous plants in winter). However, they are very expensive compared to other options.

Blank labels

Blank labels allow you to write whatever you wish on the label, but more work is involved because you need to hand write every label. It is important to use a water resistant pen or pencil otherwise the writing washes off. Another problem is that you cannot usually write as much as what would be printed. However, they are much cheaper than printed labels.

A label is the key to marketing. If it is well presented, easily read and informative it will help sell the plant. Labels with diagrams depicting sun requirement, planting method and depth, and ornamental shape are an added bonus and will help sell the plant.

When selecting labels it is important to target your clientele. A label for retail sales should be colourful, and include both botanical and common names, as well as a brief description of the plant (height, growth habit, evergreen or deciduous, soil requirements, flower colour and season, etc). A label for wholesale production often only needs the botanical name, but should be durable and weatherproof.

The type of plant grown can also influence the choice of label:
• Bare-rooted deciduous fruit trees — the customer must rely totally on the label so it is best to use a pictorial label with planting instructions and fruit characteristics. The scion variety material should also be stated.
• Herbs — many gardeners are not sure what to do with herbs so it is advisable to list the plant's potential uses as well as cultural details.
• Potted or bare rooted roses — durable coloured pictorial labels with care instructions should be included.
• Bedding plants — pictorial coloured labels are helpful, especially for newly released varieties.
• Potted conifers — coloured pictorial labels are best because they show how the plant will look in years to come.
• Cacti — a descriptive written label is usually sufficient.
• Trees and shrubs — details of mature height and width are very important.

Promotional labels should be placed in a prominent position, preferably at eye level or just below to intercept the customers' eyes as they scan the nursery. If placed too high customers will not see the labels because most people look down at the plants as they stroll through the nursery.

The labels should be weather-resistant and feature large, colourful and simple to read information. The label should not be cluttered with written text. If the plant labels are detailed then the promotional label should not contain all the same details.

Stakes, Trellises and Trainers

Stakes, trellises and trainers are used to:
1. Provide support for weak-stemmed plants until the plants have sufficient strength to stand on their own. Young growth on many plants is prone to breakage by wind gusts or the weight of the foliage when saturated from irrigation water. A stake will support the tender plant in the early stages of its life.
2. Guide growth in a particular manner. The reasons for guiding plant shape can be:
• To modify plant habit — some plants tend to grow in a horizontal pattern in the early years thereby taking more time to reach a marketable size.
• To produce an attractive plant — climbers trained onto a small trellis appear lush and are more likely to be sold than climbers tied to a single stick.
• To train plants into shapes — topiary is a technique used to sell ornamental plants to a select market group.
• To control growth — climbers look messy if the leaders are hanging from the pot.

You should determine how long the stakes and trainers are to be left with the plant. If it is only a temporary support which will be removed when the plant is planted in the garden, then a cheap, lightweight product can be used.

Containers

There is an enormous choice of containers which can be used in nurseries. The choice of container is often influenced by the cost. This is important, but the cheapest container is not necessarily the one which will grow the best plant, or help the plant sell best. Consider the following examples:

• Nurseries with automated seeding or potting machines need to use pots which are compatible with their machinery.
• Some containers (e.g. plastic bags) may be cheaper to purchase but more difficult to handle, so what is saved on the cost of the pot is lost on labour.
• Production nurseries which recycle their pots must use containers sturdy enough to be reused.
• Higher priced plants such as bonsai, Christmas trees and topiary will usually sell better if they are in a more attractive and expensive container.

Drainage
The amount of drainage in a container will determine the ratio of air to water in the root zone. The container needs to have drainage characteristics which allow the media to remain moist but not too wet.
• If all other factors are equal, a deeper pot will have better drainage characteristics than a shallower one. Overwatering is more likely to be a problem in squat pots or trays than in deep tubes.
• In some plastic pots the drainage holes are not cut cleanly. Pieces of plastic hanging over the drain holes partially or fully block these points.
• Glazed ceramic pots with only one hole in the bottom may have drainage problems.

Requirements of a plant container
• The container should have adequate drainage holes but the holes should not be large enough to allow potting media to fall out.
• The pots should be easy to separate when placed in a stack.
• The container should be strong and durable.
• The pot should produce suitable root growth, i.e. root coiling should be minimised. In this regard, tapering pots are preferable to round squat pots.
• The pots should be easy to handle (i.e. they shouldn't tip over, be too heavy, etc).

Comparing Materials

Plastic containers
Do not dry out as fast as terracotta.
Light weight.
Virtually unbreakable — they should be discarded if cracked.
Range of colours available (can be a useful marketing tool).
Relatively cheap.
New plastics are UV stabilised — this increases their lifespan.
Easy to store and clean.
Available in a range of textured finishes and styles (e.g. 'terracotta').
The basis for wholesale nurseries.

Fibreglass
Clean and durable.
May eventually discolour.
Medium lifespan.

Containers must have adequate drainage. This pot is particularly good because of the larger than normal number of drainage holes.

Terracotta

Unglazed pots absorb moisture and release water from the sides of the pot resulting in plant stress. Glazed pots may suffer from waterlogging if insufficient drainage holes exist.
Plants need to be watered more frequently.
Salting on sides may occur if mixture is kept moist.
More expensive than other containers.
Very durable, tough and long lasting.

Timber

Can rot after a year if not treated.
Natural appearance appeals to many gardeners.

Concrete

Available in almost any size.
Very heavy and expensive.
May affect pH due to lime leaching out of concrete.

Brass

Very expensive therefore usually only used indoors.
May need polishing if not treated.

Paper

Recycled paper pots are available in different sizes. They have a definite appeal to a growing niche market, but reliability of supply has been a problem in the past.

Made from recycled paper, these biodegradeable pots hold together long enough for the plant to form a strong root system. The pot is planted directly into the soil (thereby avoiding root disturbance). Eventually the pot will completely break down in the soil.

Recycled paper fibre pots.

Containers for Propagation

Propagation blocks
These units allow for sterile propagation of plants. However, they do not contain any nutrients so the plant must be potted on once roots become evident. Synthetic block units include foamed polyurethane, mineral wool (e.g Rockwool), phenolic foam and vermiculite blocks.

Compressed peat-based blocks
These are popular with both the nurseryperson and the home gardener. They come in slabs with block sections, as preformed pot strips that need to be filled with a propagation medium, or as individual compressed pots surrounded with a fine netting that expands when watered (e.g. Jiffy pots).

Plastic units
Punnet size flimsy plastic containers have been developed for germinating individual seeds. These punnets are made with either 6, 12 or 24 units. Alternatively tray size containers with 24, 40, 60 or more units are available. These are filled with the appropriate propagation medium and the seedling is grown in the container until it is large enough to be transplanted.

Plastic trays
Seeds are directly sown into the trays to achieve maximum space efficiency. However the process of transplanting can cause severe root damage to small seedlings.

Plastic pots
Pots are used for propagating larger sized plant material (i.e. cuttings and large seeds). Root disturbance is minimised when the plant is finally potted up.

Hormones

Growth regulators include hormones and other chemicals which affect the growth of plants. Certain chemical substances encourage, discourage or change the nature of growth of certain parts of the plant in preference to other parts (e.g. roots, leaves, stems, flowers, fruit). Some of these chemicals are artificial, others are natural.

The five major hormone groups are auxins, cytokinins and gibberellins (GA), absciscic acid (ABA) and ethylene.

Auxins
Auxins are involved in a variety of processes including stem growth, root formation, inhibition of lateral bud development, fruit and leaf abscission, fruit development and activating cambium cells. Of all the hormones, it is the auxins which have the greatest effect on root formation in cuttings.

The three most commonly used auxins are:
1. Indole-3-acetic acid (IAA) occurs naturally, but is less effective than IBA or NAA in promoting root growth.
2. Indolebutyric acid (IBA), an artificial auxin, is the most widely used rooting hormone. It is used on its own or in combination with NAA.
3. Napthaleneacetic acid (NAA), an artificial auxin, is used on its own or in combination with IBA.

Auxins can be applied to plants as a powder, gel or a liquid. Cuttings are frequently treated with hormones which encourage root development. The strength of hormone used will vary depending on such factors as the type of cutting being struck, the variety of plant and the application method.

Powder
The advantages of using powder are that it is easy to apply, it comes in specific concentrations, and the user doesn't need much expertise. The major disadvantage is that the powder is only available in a limited range of concentrations.

Liquid
Liquid hormones offer greater flexibility because the concentration can be varied easily by adding an appropriate liquid. The length of time which the cutting is dipped (and exposed to the hormone) can also be varied. For example, basal parts of cuttings can be soaked for 24 hours in a dilute solution (e.g. 100 ppm), or dipped in a concentrated solution (500-10,000 ppm) for about 5 seconds.

Gel
Gel remains on the cutting well. Strength can be adjusted to some degree. Other ingredients are sometimes included in the gel (e.g. vitamins).

Cytokinins

These are hormones which help with cell differentiation. Certain cytokinins applied to some plants at specific rates can help with root initiation, although more generally, cytokinins are found to inhibit root development. Cytokinins are used in tissue culture to stimulate leafy growth.

Giberellins

At high concentrations gibberellins inhibit root formation. Chemicals such as 'Alar' and 'Arrest' are commercial preparations which work by interfering with the effect of gibberellins. Gibberellins are also sometimes used as a means of overcoming seed germination inhibitors.

Paclobutryzol (e.g. 'Bonzi')

This chemical is absorbed by stems, leaves and roots. It moves to just below growing tips and inhibits gibberellin production, causing a reduction in vegetative growth and stimulation of flowering in some species. Sold as a 4 gram per litre suspension under the brand name 'Bonzi'. Its use may increase chlorophyll production, causing darker coloured foliage.

Daminozide (e.g. 'Alar')

This hormone slows down and reduces cell expansion, causing shorter internodes. It also reduces dominance of the apical tip, causing more branching. It is mainly absorbed through leaves, therefore it is best applied under slow drying conditions. The use of Alar has been banned in some countries due to health concerns.

Chlormequat (e.g. 'Cycocel')

An anti-gibberellin which reduces internode spaces on sensitive plants.

Absciscic Acid (ABA)

This naturally occurring compound plays an important role in inhibiting germination of many types of seeds, particularly those with immature embryos. ABA applications have been used to inhibit the germination of non-dormant seeds, and to offset the effects of gibberellic acid applications.

Ethylene

Ethylene is a gas produced by most plants in small quantities. When large amounts of vegetation are enclosed in a poorly ventilated space, the effects of ethylene can become significant. This is normally detected by thickening of stems. However, in some cases ethylene gas is applied to plants to promote flowering and fruit ripening. Some nurseries have used ethylene on deciduous plants to push the plants into early dormancy, enabling early winter sales. Ethylene has also been used to overcome dormancy in some seeds.

There are many other hormone treatments which are used in nurseries, but they are generally highly specific, only working on a limited number of plant varieties and only practised by nurseries which are big enough to make their use economically viable.

Mulches

Mulches are used in nurseries to control weed growth, retain soil moisture, and provide a clean surface covering.

Controlling weeds

Weeds can be a serious problem in a nursery. One weed plant can sometimes produce thousands of seeds which can then find their way into pots and plant beds throughout the nursery. The answer is to never let weeds form seeds or even better, never let weeds grow in the nursery. Thick layers of mulch along fencelines, beside buildings and on plant beds will save a lot of headaches later on.

Retaining soil moisture

Plants grown in the ground will benefit from mulching, particularly during warm weather. Plants in pots can also be mulched, although the labour involved in mulching small pots might not be worthwhile. Mulches can extend the growing season of plants, and reduce the amount of watering needed.

Mulches in retail pots

Mulches can be used to improve the appearance of container plants in the retail nursery, as well as prevent weed growth and help conserve water. Mulches used in this way include peanut shells, pine bark, sugar cane mulch, coconut fibre, and coarse sand.

Comparing Mulches

Type	Cost	Availability	Comments
Wood shavings	Cheap	Readily available in areas with sawmills	Avoid too much fine dust in the shavings; medium lasting, taking several years to decompose.
Wood chip	Medium	Readily in forestry areas and nearby cities	Can vary in quality and appearance from splinters to chunks; long lasting, having a very slow rate of decomposition.
Straw	Medium	Rural areas	Often contaminated with grass seeds; only lasts one season, decomposing relatively fast.
Lucerne hay	Medium	Better in rural areas. Available in garden packs in city nurseries	Unlikely to have weed seeds; looks good and works well; usually only lasts one season, or two if laid on thick.
Seaweed	Not sold	Collect from beaches	Needs to be washed to remove salt, then it becomes a very good mulch; a good source of micronutrients.
Leaves	Not sold	Collect from under deciduous trees in autumn	Eucalypt and conifer leaves have toxins which harm some plants.

6 Tools and Equipment

Good management of tools and equipment in the nursery involves three things:
1. Choosing the right tools and equipment.
2. Making sure tools and equipment are used and maintained properly.
3. Regular upgrading or replacement of tools and equipment.

The equipment used by staff in a nursery can make a large difference to overall productivity. A lack of spending in this area can make it impossible for staff to do an effective job, even if they are very skilled and competent. On the other hand, excessive spending in this area is a waste of money that could be better spent elsewhere.

Design
You should choose tools and equipment which are strong enough to withstand constant and sometimes heavy use. Remember, nursery tools are usually used frequently, maybe every day, whereas tools for the home garden are only used occasionally.

• Strong tools will take greater physical stress and handle heavier jobs without breaking. If you buy a cheap tool built with poor quality materials it might not last beyond the end of the first day, particularly if you are doing heavy work.
• Sharp tools put less stress on the tool, and on the user.
• Long handles give greater leverage and increased reach, putting less strain on the user's body. However long handles are sometimes impractical, especially where the tool will be used in confined spaces.
• Heavy clay or rocky soils are likely to put more strain on tools and equipment such as spades and cultivators — in these conditions you will need better quality and more heavy duty tools.
• Metal tools made with stainless steel or aluminium do not corrode like those made with other metals.

Deciding what is a good buy
Before you buy a tool or piece of equipment you need to decide whether you really need it. Too often equipment is bought simply on a whim, or because everyone else has one. Deciding to buy a tool should be based on a genuine need for that piece of equipment, for such reasons as significantly reducing workloads or the time involved in completing tasks, for safety reasons, or for improving the quality of your work.

The need for that equipment then needs to be balanced against the cost, both initial and ongoing, and the operational requirements. Is it really a worthwhile proposition? This must be decided by the following:

• Does it do the job that you require of it?
• Initial cost — how much does it cost to buy?
• Ongoing costs — this includes maintenance, parts, fuel and insurance.
• Reliability — does it break down frequently?
• Longevity — how long will it last?

- Safety to use.
- Availability of parts and servicing.

Should you rent or buy?
Often a viable alternative to buying is to rent equipment, either long or short term. These days you can hire most types of commonly used horticultural equipment (e.g. rotary hoes, tractors, chainsaws). Factors to consider include:

- How often do you use the equipment? Why buy when you can hire the equipment on the occasions you need it.
- Upfront capital costs — can you afford to buy the equipment or would it be easier to pay periodical rental or leasing costs?
- Do you have the technical expertise to keep the equipment in good working order? Good rental companies keep their equipment well maintained and serviced and will replace faulty equipment.
- In some cases the lease or rental hire may be tax deductible.

General maintenance of tools and equipment

The first thing you should do when undertaking maintenance of your tools is read the manufacturer's instructions or manuals. There may be a regular servicing or maintenance procedure required. A number of simple maintenance tasks will also help prolong the life of many tools:

1. Make sure all parts of the tool are free of foreign matter or obstructions that may impede safe and efficient use.
2. Make sure that worn or damaged parts are replaced promptly. This includes pull-start cords that might be frayed.
3. Make sure that all moving parts are well lubricated.
4. Protect any parts that are likely to rust or become corroded (e.g. paint or wipe with an oily rag).
5. Keep battery terminals free of corrosion (cover terminals with a smear of petroleum jelly) and battery levels topped up. All connections should be kept tight.
6. Make sure any oils are kept topped up, and drained and replaced at regular intervals. Oil filters on machinery should be replaced at regular intervals (follow manufacturers' recommendations).

7. Keep air cleaners clean and unblocked.
8. Keep any cutting edges properly sharpened.
9. Periodically check for and tighten any loose nuts, bolts, screws, etc.

Hand Tools

Secateurs

Every nurseryperson, whether in a production, growing-on, or retail nursery, needs a pair of secateurs. There are two main types:

1. Scissor cut — where the cutting action is achieved by two blades shearing past each other. The scissor cut is clean and doesn't bruise the plant provided the tool is kept in good condition.
2. Anvil cut — where a sharp blade comes straight down on a flat (anvil) surface. This type generally cuts more easily than the scissor type but can bruise or tear if the blade is not kept very sharp.

How to cut
All cuts should be made at a sharp angle in relation to the ground. This prevents water from collecting on the cut surface, thus reducing the likelihood of disease problems. When pruning, cuts should be made just above a node (where the leaves and/or flower stems are, or have been, attached to the plant stem). When taking cuttings, the cut should be made just below a node. This reduces the likelihood of dieback along the stem. It is also important to only cut material that is not too thick for the secateurs (ideally no more than 1-1.5 cm depending on the secateurs), otherwise you will find the cutting is a strain on both the secateurs and yourself, and the final cut is likely to be rough, torn or uneven. When using anvil secateurs, always cut down onto the anvil.

It is important to sharpen the secateur's cutting blade regularly with a sharpening stone.

On anvil types the blade should be sharpened on both sides; on scissor cut types, the blade should only ever be sharpened on the outer edge (i.e. the side which is furthest from the other blade when a cut is made).

Knives

Knives can be used for a variety of jobs in a nursery, including budding and grafting, preparing cuttings, layering, dividing plants, and pruning. Because it is a small and convenient tool many nursery workers carry a knife at all times just in case they need it for these or any other jobs. With practise, a skilled nursery worker can do most things with a knife that other gardeners might need a pair of secateurs for.

It is best to use the appropriate knife for the job at hand, and there are many different types of knives. Knives can have either fixed, folding or disposable blades.

Folding blade knives

This is the most common type of knife used in nurseries. A normal pocket knife or even a Swiss army type knife might look like a propagation knife, but they are not designed for this purpose. Different folding blade knives are designed for different tasks, so either use several different types of knives or choose a knife designed for the task which you will most commonly use it for.

Fixed blade knives

The main advantage is that the blade can't move when it is being used, so there is less chance of an accident damaging either human flesh or plant tissue.

Disposable blade knives

These come with both fixed and protractable blades. Protractable types allow a 'sectioned' blade to be slid inside a handle for safety when not being used, and slid out when needed. When the blade becomes blunt a section can be snapped off and the next piece extended for use.

Characteristics of knives

Type of Metal

Stainless steel knives are often cheaper, but do not keep their edge as well as more expensive knives made with high quality steel.

Single or double angled blade

Single angled blades are ground on one side only so that one side of the blade is sloped and the other is flat. These can only be used to cut with the flat side against the object being cut. Most specialist knives are single angled.

Double angled blades are sloped on both sides and cuts can be made any way. Knives for 'T' budding are made this way.

Weight

Knives are more efficient if most of the weight is in the handle. You can test where most of the weight is by balancing the knife on your finger.

Handle

The handle should be comfortable in the user's hand. If it is to be used for hours on end, this will become extremely important.

Attachment between blade and handle

This is a weak point and on less expensive knives the blade may become loose.

Applications

• For dividing large clumps of perennial plants, a large sturdy knife may be most appropriate. It will usually come in for rough treatment and will need to be sharpened regularly.

• For budding, a lightweight folding knife with a spatula on the end (for handling buds and lifting bark) is the traditional tool. Some nurseries find these knives are expensive and frequently go missing, so they have been replaced successfully with cheaper alternatives such as razor blades in a protractable plastic holder.

• Grafting knives are available with both curved and straight blades, although straight-edged blades are preferred.

• Pruning knives are traditionally larger knives with curved blades used for deadheading (removing spent flowers), or taking the tops off rootstocks before grafting.

Hand Saws

These have a variety of uses in the nursery, ranging from pruning and lopping to construction of such features as fences and garden furniture. The most commonly used saws in the nursery are:

Pruning saws

These generally have teeth designed to cut moist living timber; the teeth generally being larger than those on saws used for cutting furniture or construction timber. There are two types of pruning saws:

1. Straight bladed which allows variation in the type of cut according to the type and size of the material being cut.
2. Curved blade with teeth on one side. The curved saw is generally used by the experts because the curved blade allows access to restricted areas such as closely interlocking branches.

Bow saws

As the name implies, these saws are bow shaped. They are light weight, easy to use, have replacable blades, and coarse teeth which provide a fast cut when the blades are in good condition. This type of saw is popular for pruning branches that are too thick for the light pruning saws.

Carpenters' saws

There is a great variation in the types of saws used in carpentry work. Generally they have finer teeth compared to the pruning and bow saws and these are generally set to give a narrower cut. This is because they are mainly used for cutting processed timber (i.e dried, milled, heat pressed and treated timber) where a narrower, finer cut is required. These saws are predominantly straight edged with teeth only on one edge of the saw.

Simple Rules When Using Hand Saws

• Always keep the saw sharp. This makes cutting easier and gives a cleaner cut.
• Make sure you are only cutting timber. This applies particularly when cutting secondhand timber which may contain old nails, and situations where the saw may come into contact with soils, gravels or other materials that are likely to damage the saw's cutting edge.
• Always store the saws in a safe place and keep them clean. The saws are easily damaged if dropped or banged against other materials. They will quickly rust if allowed to stay moist. Incorrectly stored saws may also be a safety risk, particularly if children have access to the area where saws are left.
• Use the right saw for the job at hand. This will make the task easier for you and produce a better quality job.

Spades and shovels

Shovels are used for moving loose soil (or other loose material). The blade is cupped and at an angle inwards from the line of the handle. A shovel is not designed for digging.

Spades are used for digging and planting. The blade follows the same line as the handle.

Spades and shovels can have short or long handles, with the blade curved (i.e. a round mouth) or straight across the bottom (i.e. square mouth). Long-handled spades provide greater leverage (placing less strain on the back) and give greater reach (allowing you to dig deeper holes). They are best suited for digging holes or trenches, particularly in hard clay soils. Short-handled spades are better suited to using in confined spaces, or for digging over established garden beds with fairly loose soil.

Forks

Forks are used to cultivate or mix soil, or to move organic material about (e.g. turn over a compost heap). The prongs of a fork can either be round or flattened. Flattened prongs are more suitable for moving organic material about.

Hoes

A hoe is used to cultivate soil. A long-handled hoe which has a handle the same height as the user places least strain on the user's back. There are two main types of hoes:

1. Vertical action hoes which loosen the soil and chop under the weed. These include single prong or three prong hoes, chip hoes and draw hoes.
2. Horizontal action hoes which move through the soil just below the surface. The top of the weed is cut from the roots by the sharp blade. In the case of annual weeds, there is little if any regrowth and the weed dies. These hoes include traditional Dutch hoes and torpedo hoes.

Rakes

Rakes may vary considerably in construction and in the type of materials used. The most common types of rakes include:

• Grass and leaf rakes — These have long flat tines or teeth that lightly brush the surface you are raking, catching light loose material such as leaves and grass clippings. Some of the better quality rakes can be adjusted to change the width of the rake head to cater for differences in the size of the materials you are raking. These grass and leaf rakes are generally constructed out of metal, bamboo cane or plastic. The metal rakes generally last longer, but may rust unless they are plated. They are also more costly. The bamboo and plastic rakes don't have rust problems, and are generally cheaper than the metal ones, but are nowhere near as durable.

• Nail rakes — Generally steel teeth are riveted to a steel frame. The teeth or tines are rigid and are shorter than the grass and leaf rakes. This enables shifting of heavier material and also for the rake to have a cultivator-like effect on loose soils. If incorrectly used, the teeth may become loose.

• Single piece rake heads — Generally formed from a single piece of carbon steel, sometimes from moulded plastic. This type has similar functions to the nail rake. Teeth size, shape and number varies according to the type of work to be undertaken. For example you may have 10, 12, 14 or 16 teeth depending on whether you are raking fine or coarse gravel, asphalt or soil. Both nail and single piece rakes usually have sockets welded to the frame for the easy attachment of wooden handles.

Snap lock tools

There are several modular tool systems with a range of heads that can be connected to the one handle as required. Available heads include rakes, hoes and cultivators, aerators, seed sowers and pruners.

Major advantages of this system are the space which is saved in storing tools and the flexibility of being able to vary the length of handle on a tool head. The main disadvantage is that there is greater wear and tear on the handle and the locking mechanism than on any individual head.

Wheelbarrows

When buying a wheelbarrow make sure the main centre of balance is over the wheel and not on your arms, and that you have plenty of leg room when wheeling the barrow. Choose a solid, well constructed wheelbarrow. A well built wheelbarrow will last for several decades if properly maintained. Keep tyres pumped up, grease all moving parts, wash out soil or rubbish after use and store out of the weather. If these things are not done you will be lucky to keep a barrow in use for more than 5 years.

Nursery trolleys

Nursery trolleys are an essential item in every nursery. They are two, three or four-wheeled trolleys with a wide, shallow tray which is primarily used for moving plants around the nursery. Most trolleys will hold both pots and seedling trays. The trolley tray is covered with a metal mesh to allow water to freely drain away when plants in the trolley are watered before unloading.

Several trolleys should be conveniently located in production areas for nursery workers and in sales areas for customers to transport their selected plants in.

Multi-level nursery trolley. This trolley can be used to move more plants than most trailers or barrows, provided the plants are not too tall.

Roof-supported trolley system for moving stock inside a greenhouse.

Hand trolleys

Upright hand trolleys are useful for moving many things about the nursery including boxes of materials (e.g. chemicals, pots, tools) when delivered and large planter tubs when a forklift or tractor isn't available. They are particularly useful in retail nurseries or at shows and exhibitions where a small upright trolley is more manoeuvrable than a larger nursery trolley.

Clothing

Some nurseries supply staff with selected items of clothing. This decision might be forced upon the nursery by 'award' regulations, or it may be taken as a management decision for one or another of the following reasons:

• To present a particular image. This is of particular benefit for staff who are frequently being seen by

customers (e.g. sales staff, office staff, sales reps, staff manning trade displays at shows). Something as simple as T-shirts, windcheaters or caps bearing the business name and logo will be of great value.
• To ensure staff wear clothing which is safe. This can include non-slip footwear in slippery places, tight fitting clothing near machinery, hats to protect against sunburn or skin cancer, and protective gear against chemicals.
• To improve productivity. Raincoats and gum boots may encourage staff to work in wet weather.
• For staff morale. Providing certain items of clothing can be a way of giving staff a reason to be a little happier with their job, without having given them a pay increase.

Machinery

Machines are tools which have moving parts usually powered by an electric or petrol engine. Machinery can make a dramatic difference to the amount of work a nursery can do. Machines enable simple jobs like cultivation, spraying and moving plants about to be carried out faster and with a minimum of physical strain on the staff. More sophisticated and expensive machines can even carry out routine nursery work such as seeding and potting.

Vehicles

One of the biggest expenses for a nursery (after the cost of the land and buildings) is a vehicle or vehicles to transport plants. Retail nursery staff will need to travel to wholesalers to buy plants or make deliveries of plants to customers. Wholesale nurseries will need to make deliveries to customers. New small nurseries can often delay this major expense by modifying a tandem trailer and pulling it with the family car. This is generally only a temporary measure though. A tandem trailer or truck which is used to transport plants must be modified to do the following:

• Protect the plants from wind. A canopy (preferably one that will totally enclose the trailer) must be provided.
• Hold the optimum number of plants. This is often achieved by creating shelving. You will need to pay

particular attention to the height between shelves. Ideally shelving should be adjustable so that shelving heights can be adjusted according to the plants you are carrying.
• Take the weight of a full load. There can be a lot of soil in a full load of plants. You should calculate this weight and obtain a trailer or truck which can easily deal with the load. If pulling a trailer with a car, make sure the car is capable (rated) of pulling the trailer when fully loaded.

Mulchers

Mulchers are useful in nurseries for the disposal of prunings and in some isolated locations can be used to provide organic material for potting mixes. If the mulcher is to be used in this way, a relatively powerful mulcher is needed to chip the material into small pieces and the chipped material must be composted before it is added to the potting media.

Only plant material should be put into the the machine to be shredded. Other material can damage the blades and other working parts. These machines are noisy so hearing protection should be worn and the manufacturer's safety instructions should be followed closely. These machines should only be operated by adults.

Cultivators

Rotary hoes and cultivators are used to prepare soil beds for growing stock plants and in-ground production. This type of equipment is very important in advanced tree nurseries, bulb farms or any other nurseries where plants are to be field grown then dug up for sale.

Rotary hoes are used to loosen the soil, providing a well cultivated tilth. These machines can be self-propelled or power take-off driven, and they can be tractor mounted or pedestrian operated. The self-propelled machines are generally driven by petrol engines and they move forward by rubber-tyred drive wheels or by using the rotating blades to pull the machine. Most require a reasonably strong person to operate them properly.

For tractor-mounted machines the large rotors are powered by the power take-off unit. The rotor is a shaft onto which a series of L-shaped blades are bolted which dig into and turn over the soil. Around the rotor is a shield that protects the operator from flying debris and soil clods. The blades rotate in the direction of forward travel, slicing into the ground and throwing the soil into the other blades or against the shield where it is pulverised.

The small self-propelled units are useful in tight conditions and down to soil depths of 15 to 20 cm, while the tractor operated versions are more suitable for larger areas and where greater depths of cultivation are required.

Tractor-drawn cultivators come in a wide range of types. Some mix the soil, others cultivate without having much effect on the soil profile. Check the equipment available and be sure to get the appropriate cultivator for the intended use.

Tree Spades

These are specialised tractor-mounted attachments designed to help lift trees which have been grown to an advanced size in nursery rows.

Soil Mixing Equipment

Cement mixers, small or large, are sometimes used for mixing potting media in those nurseries which

Eight-horsepower mulching machine. Mulchers are useful for the disposal of prunings, and for supplying limited amounts of mulch. Commercial nurseries would generally require a more powerful machine, especially if large quantities of mulches are required for potting mixes and for mulching display and stock beds.

make their own mixes. In some larger nurseries large amounts of soils, composts, mulches or growing media are mixed and/or transported using a front-end loader. Ideally these materials should only be mixed and stored on a clean surface such as concrete so that they are not contaminated by soil particles, and soil-borne pest and diseases from underlying soil.

Conveyor Belts

Conveyor belts can be used to move plants away from work areas to growing-on areas. They are not viable in small nurseries, but some large nurseries have found that they can contribute towards improved productivity.

Potting Machines

Potting plants is extremely labour intensive and many nurseries have found that automated potting machines have signicantly improved nursery efficiency. There are a number of different models available, including machines which do the following:

1. Controllable volume system — the amount of soil which is poured into the pot can be controlled by pushing a foot pedal or hand button. Soil will continue to be delivered until the foot pedal or button is released.
2. Pre-set volume — the volume of soil is pre-set, although this can be changed for different-sized pots and plants.
3. Combination of the above — more sophisticated machines can be set to either method.

The pots can be moved along a conveyor belt or set on rotating benches. The soil may be fed through a central hopper or along a conveyor belt.

Potting machine rates
Statistics given vary from 200 pots per man hour to 500 per man hour, potting into rigid 7.8 cm pots, and including all operations (i.e. bringing in soil mix, cuttings, potting, placing down and watering in, but excluding taking the filled pots back to the nursery rows).

Total labour for potting expressed in minutes per plant (potting into rigid pots)

Container size	Average (mins)	Best (mins)
2 litre general shrubs	0.93	0.74
3 litre general shrubs	0.98	0.78
2–3 litre climbers	1.06	0.89
2 litre clematis	1.16	0.93

(These figures do not include bringing soil to the potting bench, or taking away potted plants.)

Source: *Container Plant Manual*, J. Edmonds, published by Grower Books.

Seeding Machines

There is a range of seeding machines used by nurseries. Most feed seeds into soil or potting media by a vacuum mechanism (e.g. seeds are picked up when a vacuum is created, then dropped in a desired position when the vaccuum is disengaged).

Using these machines, plants grown in the field may be direct sown into nursery rows. Plants grown in containers can be grown by using a seeding machine and a compatible transplanting machine. Many annual and vegetable seedlings are propagated into 'plugs' using this type of equipment. Seedling nurseries have been known to effectively halve their labour costs by using this type of machinery, and despite the initial high cost of the machines, the cost benefits have been enormous.

Sprayers

Sprayers are used for applying chemical sprays (insecticides, fungicides and herbicides) and liquid fertilisers. It is advisable to use a different sprayer for each type of chemical. Herbicide residues left from previous spray jobs can contaminate insecticides and damage plants being sprayed for insects.

There are many different types of sprayers available including:

1. Disposable spray guns — plastic bottles with a pump action handle on top. Many chemicals are sold as a ready-to-use spray in this type of bottle. Refills can be bought to screw onto the top of the spray mechanism.

Knapsack sprayer. All nurseries should have at least two of these: one for weedicides only (clearly marked 'Weedicides Only'), the other for use with pesticides.

2. Pressurised back or shoulder pack units — a container which can be pressurised with a flexible hose and connecting spray nozzle. The unit is pumped by hand to raise the pressure in the container. A trigger is used to release pressure and spray as required.

3. Motorised sprayers — a container which holds the chemical is pumped from a motorised pump and out through a spray nozzle.

Irrigation Equipment

Water is generally applied in nurseries by one of the following systems:
1. Hand watering
2. Moveable sprinklers
3. Fixed sprinkler/watering systems (manually operated)
4. Semi-automatic watering systems
5. Fully automatic watering systems

Hand watering

There is no doubt that watering by hand with a good quality watering can is the best way to water plants. It allows the nurseryperson to deliver the water where it is needed, in the required quantity, which may vary from plant to plant. However, hand watering is a very expensive way to water and is only economically viable in special circumstances.

Nurseries use watering cans for various tasks. When used to water in cuttings immediately after planting or seed immediately after sowing, the can must deliver a gentle and even supply of water. Inexpensive watering cans can sometimes drip (not always when you first buy them), or lose their rose, damaging the pot or tray you are watering. Cheap alternatives are simply not worth the risk.

Watering cans are also used to water particularly valuable plants, or in situations where it is important to not get water on foliage or flowers. High value plants such as bonsai or rare plant varieties may be watered this way. Some nurseries which are renowned for growing top quality plants such as african violets or pelargoniums use hand watering either all of the time, or perhaps only for a period prior to selling the plant. This way they avoid marks on foliage or flowers.

Sprinklers

Sprinklers are a much cheaper way of watering plants, and for most plants it is the most appropriate way of watering in a nursery. There are two types of sprinkler heads:

1. Spray head
This head does not have moving parts. Water is sprayed over the total area to be covered all at once, whether that be in a full circle, a part circle (i.e. wedge shape), or some other shape. These sprinklers cover relatively small areas.

2. Rotating head
This sprinkler has moving parts. It rotates and squirts out a stream of water in one or several directions, spreading the water as it moves.

The type and placement of sprinkler heads is critical to achieving a uniform coverage of water. Different types of sprinkler heads will deliver water at different rates and covering different areas. The

Irrigation with overhead sprinklers.

precipitation rate is normally expressed as inches or millimetres per hour. The precipitation rate can vary by up to 400% from one area to another covered by the same sprinkler system. This can mean plants in one area may be severely underwatered while plants in another area may be severely overwatered.

A sprinkler will often not distribute water evenly over the full radius which it covers. Water is usually distributed evenly over the 35% of the radius closest to the sprinkler head, but the amount of water distributed beyond this point decreases. The distribution of water to the outer edge of the radius can drop even more if there is a wind blowing. (Prevailing winds may need to be considered when deciding where to place sprinkler heads.)

Sprinklers water a circular-shaped area (or an oval shape if it is windy). If sprinklers which water a radius of 10 metres are placed 20 metres apart, the outer edges of water cover from each sprinkler may meet each other, but there will be patches between where there will be no water cover. If the sprinklers are moved closer together, both sprinkler heads will be applying water to some areas (i.e. there

Drip irrigation. Pots with individual drippers are an efficient but expensive watering system. In most cases it is only appropriate to use with higher cost plants. It is used here on grafted grevilleas.

will be an overlap), but other areas will receive cover from only one head.

Smaller sprinklers and heads which only water part of a circle (ie. half or quarter) can be used effectively for watering odd shaped places.

Trickle irrigation

Trickle irrigation provides a slow dripping of water at one point. Trickle methods conserve water (i.e. make better use of water resources) compared to conventional sprinkler irrigation, particularly when delivering water to garden beds, row crops (e.g. advanced tree crops in the open ground) or individual plants in large containers. It can also be useful for watering hanging baskets, and for watering plants which have delicate foliage.

Although the design of systems varies greatly, the basic components of all trickle systems include an automatic controlling device, a pressure regulator (to ensure water pressure is even between droppers), filter, control valves and drippers.

Problems with trickle irrigation:
• In sandy soil, water moves straight down (there is little horizontal movement in the soil).

• Salt can build up (shown by a white caking) in the area where the water is applied.
• There is some research to indicate that root development is restricted to the wetted area, particularly with larger plants.

If trickle irrigation systems are to operate without serious blockage of the fine water outlets, some periodic maintenance is necessary. Generally this maintenance consists of cleaning filters, flushing the system, and chlorination of the system.

Trickle irrigation has the following advantages:
• Water conservation
Water is directed exactly where the plant needs it most — the plant roots. Loss of water from wind and excess runoff is minimised, giving a saving on water rates and conserving increasingly scarce fresh water supplies.
• Saves labour
Although trickle systems are initially time consuming to set up and occasionally require some ongoing maintenance, trickle systems are permanent fixtures which are fully automated.
• Doesn't get water where it is not wanted
People, paths, furniture, etc. close to the water outlet don't get wet when the system is on. In nurseries

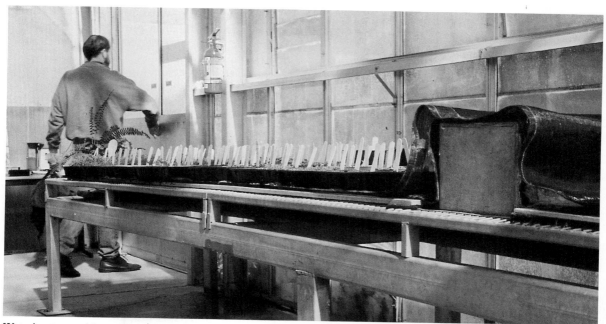

Watering trays with capillary matting. Water soaks through the absorbent mat, from the box on the bench to underneath the plant trays.

this means that work schedules don't have to be interrupted by spray from overhead sprinklers.
• Reduces weed growth and diseases
Weeds have less chance of germinating because the area of moist soil is reduced.
• Reduces diseases
Trickle systems don't wet the foliage and flowers. Wet foliage and flowers are more susceptible to diseases.

Capillary watering

This involves water soaking up into the bottom of plant pots or trays. Capillary watering supplies a constant supply of water to plants without needing to wet the foliage.
There are two main ways this is done:
1. Capillary matting
A water-absorbent mat is laid on a surface (sometimes with one end immersed into a container of water). Plants stood on top will absorb water through the drainage holes and the water will then soak upwards into the potting mix.
2. Water well pots
A reservoir (usually a saucer) of water is attached to the bottom of a pot. As the plant uses water and the potting mix dries, it is replenished by water soaking up through the bottom of the pot.

Automatic Systems

Irrigation can be controlled automatically by sensing devices (which switch the water on when it is needed) or by time clocks which switch the water on at the time of day when you tell it to water and for the length of time which you tell it to water for.
While they are an excellent way to save labour and time, it is important that you do not over rely on automatic systems. Automatic systems can require resetting as conditions change from time to time throughout the year. They can also break down, and watering might be missed without you noticing. You should frequently check their operation and the way they are affecting the plants.

Pumps

There are many different types of pumps used by nurseries. They are used for pumping water to the plants, and pressurising sprayers to spray chemicals.
Gravity should be utilised in all possible ways before resorting to the use of a pump (i.e. if water supply can be achieved by gravity being used to achieve water flow, this is preferable to using a pump).
Before deciding on what type of pump to use in a system, you must first determine the flow of water required in a peak demand situation (i.e. what rate do you want water to be supplied when the pump is working at its maximum capacity?). Pressure created by the pump must be sufficient to lift water from the lowest point of water supply to the highest point which water is being applied to.
Pumps are usually either:
1. Shallow well pumps, used to raise water up to 7.5 metres. The pumping mechanism uses suction to lift the water from a level below the level of the pumping mechanism, or
2. Deep well pumps, used to raise water heights greater than 7.5 metres. This type has the pump actually immersed in the water which is being pumped.

Pumping Mechanisms
The three different pumping mechanisms are piston, centrifugal and turbine.

Piston pumps   Also called 'force' or 'reciprocating' pumps, these work on a plunger principle (i.e. a plunger or piston moving inside a sealed cylinder creates the pressure).
• Double action piston pump delivers water on both the forward and backward strokes.
• Simple windmill pump delivers water only on one stroke.

Characteristics of piston pumps:
• A high pressure is produced.
• Because water is delivered in surges, an air chamber is incorporated to even out the flow.
• Flow is smaller than other types of pumps.
• Excellent suction performance up to 7.5 metres in height.
• Higher maintenance requirement than other pumps.
• Transmission needs to be organised for suitable speed reductions to be achieved.

Centrifugal pumps   Pumping is achieved by a rotating disc or wheel with attached blades (i.e. vanes) which continuously sling water as the wheel rotates. These pumps are commonly used and there are many models designed for many purposes. It is important to select the right one for the right purpose.

Turbine pumps These work by water rotating an impeller inside a bowl.

Pump flow is measured in litres per second or litres per minute as follows:
1 litre per second = 60 litres per minute = 13.2 gallons per minute.
1 gallon per minute = 4.6 litres per minute.

Pressure is measured in either metre head of water, or in kilopascals (kPa). One pound per square inch (p.s.i.) = approximately 7 kilopascals.
A pump operating at 350 kPa is the same as one operating at 50 p.s.i.
1 kPa = 34 feet of water = 11 metres of water.

Water treatment

If water quality is poor due to physical, chemical or biological contaminants, it may be necessary to treat water before using it in a nursery. Some nurseries collect and recycle waste or runoff water, then reuse it. It is likely that this will become a legal obligation for at least some nurseries in the future.

Scheduling Irrigation

Wilting point is the point at which the soil is so dry that the plant begins to wilt. Field capacity is the point at which the soil is holding as much water as it can without excess water simply draining away and being lost.
    The zone between wilting point and field capacity is important because you should aim to keep moisture levels within this zone.
    Generally plants take most of their requirements from the upper half of the root zone and as a result only about half of the available water is used. Irrigation is therefore required when approximately half of the available water is used up. The amount of water to be applied to plants is half of the available water in the root zone when the soil is at field capacity.
    Irrigation applications are timed according to how quickly the plants use the available moisture. This is dependant on climatic conditions and the availability of nutrients. The rate at which water is supplied by irrigation is important due to soil infiltration rates, or the rate at which water will pass into the soil. If water is supplied at a rate greater than the soil can absorb it, then runoff may occur resulting in a loss of water.
    The following table gives an indication of infiltration rates for some soils.

Soil type	Infiltration rate
Coarse sand	2500 mm/hr
Sandy loam	20–100 mm/hr
Loam	10–20 mm/hr
Silty loam	5–10 mm/hr
Clay loam	1–5mm/hr

The ideal situation is where application rates are equal to infiltration rates. Infiltration rates can also be affected greatly by compaction which causes reduction in pore space and hence space available for water and its passage.

Before scheduling irrigation you should know:
• precipitation rate of the sprinkler system
• infiltration rate of the soil
• available water held in the soil per cm of soil depth
• average daily evaporation
• root depth

The length of time you operate a sprinkler station for will depend upon:
• the rate of water delivered by the system (the precipitation rate); and
• the rate at which water is absorbed into the soil (the infiltration rate).

Pulse Watering

This can be used to obtain a deeper penetration of water where water loss through runoff is excessive. Pulse watering involves shorter but more frequent irrigation. For example, instead of watering for half an hour daily, it might involve a 5 minute watering followed by a 15 minute break, then another 5 minutes of watering and another 15 minute break, etc. This might be repeated twice more, giving a total of 20 minutes of watering.

7 Buildings and Structures

Nurseries use buildings to store things, to work in and to grow plants. Greenhouses, shadehouses and other structures are used to create better environments for plants. Other buildings are used as offices, lunch rooms, potting sheds, propagation areas, dispatch areas or to provide security and protection from the weather for tools and equipment.

Greenhouses

Greenhouses are normally used for one or more of the following:
• To propagate new plants by providing the ideal conditions for seeds to germinate or cuttings to initiate root growth.
• To grow tropical plants in cooler climates.
• To protect plants which are cold or frost sensitive over winter.
• To grow vegetables, cut flowers or berry fruits out of season or faster than what might be achieved outside.
• To grow nursery container plants over winter.
• To provide a contained growing environment in which CO_2 enrichment is carried out to promote increased yields.
• To provide a contained isolated growing environment for plant breeding or quarantine purposes.

There may be other uses, but these are the main ones.

Types of greenhouses

There are many different types of greenhouses available today. Each type has advantages and disadvantages. Generally speaking, the old adage applies, 'You get what you pay for'. Some of the more expensive greenhouses can last a lifetime and will in many respects do a better job, however, the initial cost may be a deterrent.

Small plastic-covered tent over a propagating bed. In particularly cold climates, this provides extra protection at night and increases humidity.

Multispan greenhouse with roll-up sides.

The three most common designs for commercial greenhouses are:

1. Gable — This type is generally used with the inflexible covering materials such as glass. The straight-sided walls make it easy to use the entire floor space.

2. Igloo — The hemispherical cross-section makes this the best shape for light transmission (less sunlight is reflected). This type is also the most efficient in terms of the amount of covering material required and volume enclosed. However, the curved sides make it difficult to use the space as fully as straight-walled greenhouses. Only the more flexible materials such as coreflute/polyflute and PVC film can be used on igloos.

3. Raised arch — This is a compromise between the gable and igloo types. Light transmission is better than the gable type, but not as good as for the igloo, however the straight sides of the raised arch make it easier to work in than the igloo. Only flexible materials (e.g. PVC film) can be used to cover the curved roof section.

Multispan versus Single span Greenhouses

Multispan

Advantages
Less covering material required.
Easier to heat overall area.
Most efficient use of ground space.

Disadvantages
Harder to control heat than for single span.
Easy for pests and diseases to spread.

Single span

Advantages
Easier to control heating.
Easier to control pests.
Provide more specific growing conditions for different types of plants.

Disadvantages
Less efficient use of ground space.
More structural materials required.

Greenhouses and shadehouses are now commonly available in kit form for the home gardener. These are sometimes used as a starter greenhouse for backyard nursery growers, or for housing displays in retail nurseries. On a full commercial scale these structures can be readily obtained in a wide variety of sizes and styles, often in multiples of a basic sized unit (e.g. 6 x 4 m, 10 x 4 m), or they can be made to order.

Construction method

Shortwall The transparent material covers the roof and the upper part of the sides. The lower parts are covered with non-transparent material such as timber or brick.

Longwall The transparent material covers all of the walls and all of the roof.

Tunnel The framework is made from half-circle metal hoops arranged in a row to form a tunnel shape. Transparent material is laid over this framework. (PVC film or more solid plastics are the most commonly used materials.)

Lean-To A structure attached to the side of another building (e.g. a house). The other building provides one side wall for the greenhouse.

Framing Materials

Metal

Aluminium frames are popular because they resist rusting, they are relatively strong and are light weight. Galvanised iron or steel are also used, although over time corrosion can become a problem.

Glass goes well with metal framing. PVC film and other plastics can deteriorate if in direct contact with metal (e.g. metal will get very hot in summer, and

the sections of PVC film touching metal will crack or tear much sooner than other parts).

The strength of the various metals allows use of structural members which have smaller cross-sections than timber used for the same task. This results in reduced shading in comparison to timber. Metal frames are readily obtained in preformed shapes that can make assembly very easy.

Timber

Timber does not heat up like metal, but it may rot, particularly in the humid environment of a greenhouse. Some treated timbers will last for many years, however it is important to check that the materials used in treating the wood are non-toxic to plants.

Pests such as mealy bug may breed in timber. Timber is very readily worked with (i.e. it easy to cut, nail and drill), and is very useful for constructing non-standard sized greenhouses.

Covering Materials

When choosing covering materials for a growing structure it is important to consider:
- Insulation (the materials' ability to hold heat in).
- Light transmission (how much of the light

Multispan glasshouse.

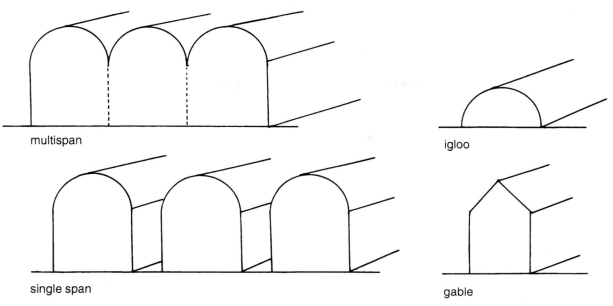

multispan

igloo

single span

gable

Different types of greenhouses

reaching the greenhouse will travel through the covering). Some materials will become increasingly opaque over time, reducing the amount of light being transmitted.
• Cost (some materials are far more expensive to buy).
• Lifespan (length of time until the material needs to be replaced).
• Flexibility (more flexible materials are easier to build with).
• Durability (the amount of wear and tear they can withstand).

Glass
Glass is very rigid and can't be used on tunnel type structures. It is one of the best materials for insulation, light transmission and durability (it will last 50 to 100 years), but is the most expensive. It is more resistant to storms than most other materials, but can be dangerous and difficult to clean up if it is broken. It is more readily cleaned than most other covering materials (cleaning is normally only required for some of the longer lasting materials).

Coreflute/polyflute
This is a semi-rigid material, with two layers of plastic joined together by corrugated ribbing.

Insulation qualities are good, and light transmission is good but less so than glass or PVC film. Cost is reasonably inexpensive given that it will normally last for at least ten years. It has good resistance to inclement weather, and won't shatter like glass. Small puncture holes can be readily patched. It comes in large sheets or rolls and is easy to work with. The large size of the sheeting also reduces heat loss. It is flexible enough to be used on tunnel and arch type greenhouses. Algae can sometimes be a problem on and between the sheets.

Corrugated PVC sheet
A semi-rigid material of moderate to high cost, average durability, and good insulation. Light transmission is lower than most of the alternatives.

Polycarbonate
Longlasting, very strong, expensive. Available in clear or smoky grey sheets, or corrugated. Excellent light transmission, flexible and easy to work with. It tends to collect dust.

Corrugated Fibreglass Sheet
Semi rigid, similar to acrylic coated PVC sheet but more expensive. Light transmission not as good as alternatives (i.e. glass, coreflute, PVC film). It tends to become yellow and brittle with age.

PVC film
A very flexible, inexpensive material. It has a short lifespan (normally a few years) and is susceptible to damage from hail, winds, storms, etc. There are many different types of films — some have reasonable insulation and good light transmission properties, others are poor. Some have inhibitors to reduce the effect of UV light, which is the major contributor to the breakdown of most of these films. Condensation forming on the inside can result in dripping (on plants and you), and can lead to heat loss.

In areas where damage from weather is not a major problem PVC film can be the most cost-efficient covering material. It is sometimes used as a double cover to improve insulation, but some light transmission is lost. These films can flap noisily in the wind, particularly if poorly erected.

Reinforced PVC film
This PVC film has woven thread embedded in the plastic to provide reinforcement — this improves its strength and durability. There is slightly less light transmission which at times can be an advantage, depending on the type of plants being grown. It is more expensive than standard PVC film.

Deciding what you need
When deciding which type of structure would best suit your needs keep these few simple points in mind:
1. Plant growth requirements — for example, do you really need a glasshouse or will a shadehouse be adequate?
2. Space — how much space is available for setting up your structure, or how much space is required for the number of plants you wish to grow?
3. Cost — how much are you prepared to spend?
4. Product availability — is it easy to get and are replacement materials easy to obtain?
5. Ease of construction — do you have the necessary expertise to build one of these structures, or will you have to pay someone else to build it for you? Is a kit the best option?
6. Lifespan — how much effort are you prepared to spend on repairs and maintenance?
7. Local bylaws — are there any regulations that govern use of such structures in your area, for example size limitations, type of construction, or siting restrictions?

Siting greenhouses

Consider the following:
• Is the site on a slope or is it flat? Too steep a site will make it impossible to build the greenhouse unless it is terraced.
• Is the site in sun or shade? A windbreak will be useful, but take care to avoid shading the greenhouse.
• What sort of base is going to be used (e.g. concrete, gravel)?
• What sort of soil is the greenhouse going to be built on? A sandy soil will give good drainage from watering, but a clay soil will not. You may need to install a drainage system before construction.

Orientation
It is best to orient the greenhouse with the ridge running east to west. This will maximise the amount of sunlight received and reduce shading. However, the orientation may be governed by the space that you have available.

Benching

Benches enable you to raise plants off the greenhouse floor, keeping them away from disease and often in better light. They also make work easier for staff (less bending!). A tiered system of benches usually provides more useable space than if you were to only use the floor.

Benches can be made out of metal, wood or plastic. The surface of a bench should drain freely. Wooden benches should be treated with preservative to prevent rotting and infestations by pests such as white ants and mealy bug. Capillary matting (i.e. a continually moist, absorbent material, sold by some greenhouse companies) will help reduce the need for watering if used on a bench.

Cleanliness in the greenhouse

The greenhouse can be isolated from the outside environment, hence the likelihood of pests and diseases entering the greenhouse is reduced. However, if pests and diseases do get inside, the warm, moist environment can be conducive to their rapid spread.
• Good ventilation will help provide some control.

Wire mesh greenhouse bench provides excellent drainage.

• Sterilise the house annually.
• Pasteurise beds in greenhouses annually (steam at 60–71°C for 30 minutes or use chemicals such as methyl bromide).

Problems with greenhouses

The following are some of the most common problems experienced with growing plants in greenhouses:
• Overheating — on a hot day, the greenhouse temperature can rise very quickly and overheat plants before you realise it. Ventilation and shading are used to keep the temperature down. In some locations a shadecloth covering may be required during summer months.
• Frost damage — a severe frost will penetrate through the sides and roof of even the best greenhouses. If the house isn't heated, keep your most tender plants in the centre of the house away from the walls.
• Plants drying out — the extra warmth in a greenhouse means that plants in pots dry out faster and need watering more often.

Coldframes

Coldframes are in effect mini-greenhouses. They are most commonly used by home gardeners, but can also be effectively used in a nursery. The frame can be used to grow seedlings, propagate cuttings, and provide a protected environment for budding and grafting.

The frame is a simple structure, usually box-like with a hinged top. The walls of the frame can be either a transparent material such as polyflute, or non-transparent such as timber. The top is at an angle (so water can run off) and can be opened and closed for access and to allow air in, depending on the weather. Opening and closing the lid also controls the temperature and humidity. The angle of the lid faces nearly at right angles to the sun, in an easterly or northerly direction. The back wall faces west or south.

The advantage of a coldframe over a glasshouse is that you get greater coverage of ground space using fewer materials. They can be moved around to the best spot, or changed from a sunny position to shade depending on the season. They can be

Timber slats used for shading a cold frame in summer. During winter the bed is covered with glass. (Geneva Botanic Gardens Nursery)

designed so that new frames can be attached to previously built frames.

The disadvantages are that you are working at ground level and not at a bench, and because of the smaller internal volume, the frame can heat up and cool down faster, and so it needs to be watched more closely.

Shadehouses

Nurseries use shadehouses as a staging area to ease plants into a harsher environment when they are taken from a greenhouse, or to grow plants in a protected environment. They are used to protect plants from hot sun, frost, wind or excessively bright light.

Shadehouses are also used to provide a permanent growing area for plants which prefer shade and will eventually be grown in shaded positions in a garden (e.g. impatiens, ferns, some orchids, azaleas, and rainforest plants like gingers, monsteria and philodendrons).

Shadehouses can be covered in materials such as wooden slats, or shadecloth. These allow the passage of rainwater (reducing the impact of heavy rain) and air, but reduce the amount of light reaching the plants beneath.

Shadecloth now comes in many colours (e.g. pale blue, sandstone, brown or white) as well as the traditional green and black. In terms of plant growth, green is the least desirable colour as the translucent green fibres make the light slightly green. Plants are least efficient at photosynthesising in the green wavelength of light. In addition the particular green used does not blend in with natural leaf greens. Black is perhaps the colour which is least noticeable. White shadecloth is good for growing plants because although they are protected from direct sunlight they are still growing in relatively bright conditions.

Shadecloth is available in different grades in terms of light transmission, (e.g. 50% and 70% shade are common). The stronger shade is used in hotter climates and to grow shade-loving plants like ferns in summer. The rating of shade is determined at right angles to the light, and so depending on the angle at which the sun hits the cloth, you will commonly get more shade than the stated amount. With some plants this may mean that they are not getting enough light. Shadecloth (50%) can also be used as a windbreak material.

Environmental Control in Greenhouses

Nurseries manipulate the growth of plants by using different types of equipment to control growth factors such as temperature, light intensity and duration, humidity and in some instances even the levels of different gases in the air.

Environmental factors which influence plant growth
1. Atmospheric temperature — the air.
2. Root zone temperature — in the soil or growing media in which the plant roots are growing in.
3. Water temperature — the water which you irrigate the plants with.

Innovative use of shadecloth over a nursery row. (Canning Plant Farm, Perth, Western Australia)

4. Light conditions — shaded, full light, dark.

5. Atmospheric gas — plants give off oxygen but take in carbon dioxide during photosynthesis. Plants will take in some oxygen during respiration (converting stored foods such as glucose into energy) and release some carbon-dioxide, but in an enclosed environment the amount of carbon-dioxide in the atmosphere will soon diminish.

6. Air movement — mixes gases and evens out temperature fluctuations.

7. Atmospheric moisture — humidity.

8. Root zone moisture — water levels in the soil or media.

Plant Needs

Every variety of plant has specific needs and tolerances with respect to the environment in which it grows. The horticulturist talks about 'optimum' conditions; 'tolerated' conditions; and conditions which are 'not tolerated'.

Optimum conditions are the conditions in which the plant grows best. Some plants have a wide optimum range, perhaps growing just as well at any temperature from 18 to 28°C. Other plants have a narrow optimum range (e.g. growing well at temperatures from 24–26°C).

Tolerated conditions are the conditions under which the plant will survive, but not necessarily grow (e.g. a plant might have an optimum temperature range of 20–26°C, and a tolerant range of −2 to 49°C.

Not tolerated — if conditions go outside the tolerated range, the plant will die, or at least be damaged.

Note: These principles apply equally to light, moisture, and other environmental conditions for a plant.

Temperature Control

Principles behind temperature control in greenhouses:

• Heat is lost by conduction (through walls and roof), infiltration (warm air being lost from the greenhouse) and radiation (heat radiating from warm objects inside the house).

• A central heating system is more efficient than localised heaters. Localised heaters are cheap to purchase but more expensive to run.

• Emergency heaters (back-ups) are desirable.

• Air circulation and distribution of heat from source points (e.g. heaters) is critical to ensure even temperature control. Air fans are sometimes used to distribute heat. Large diameter polythene tubes with outlet holes are also sometimes used.

• Any thermostats should be at a height and position which reflects the temperature of the growing tip of plant being grown. They should be housed in a light-reflecting box, where they will not be abnormally affected by the cooling effect of watering, excessive heating or sunlight.

• Heat requirements can be reduced by installing a second covering (e.g. PVC film) over the greenhouse.

• Exhaust fan placement is important. When walls are less than 4.5 metres apart, fans in adjacent walls should alternate (i.e. they should not be opposite).

Greenhouse temperatures can be controlled in several ways:

• The sun will warm the green house during the day. This effect varies according to the time of year, time of day and the weather. The way the greenhouse is built and the materials used in construction will also influence the house's ability to catch and store heat from the sun.

• Heaters can be used to add to the heat in a house. The heater must have the ability to replace heat at the same rate at which it is being lost to the outside so that desired temperatures can be maintained.

• Vents and doors can be opened to let cool air into the greenhouse, or closed to stop warm air from escaping.

• Shadecloth can be drawn over the house to reduce the amount of sunlight being transmitted into the greenhouse. Greenhouse paints (whitewash) can be applied in spring for the same effect. The type of paint used is normally one which will last the summer, but wash off with weathering to allow sunlight in winter.

• Coolers (blowers etc), exhaust fans, and watering or misting systems can be used to lower temperature.

• Water storage, or rock beds, under the floor or benches of a glasshouse can act as a buffer to temperature fluctuations.

• Hot beds used to heat root zone areas will also help heat the greenhouse.

• Thermal blankets can be drawn across the top of greenhouses at night, usually by means of a small hand-operated winch to trap in heat gained during the day.

Heat loss

An important consideration in temperature control is the heat lost through the walls and the roof of the house. Different types of covering materials have differing levels of ability to retain heat. Heat is normally measured in BTUs (British Thermal Units). The table below provides some insight into the respective qualities of different materials.

Covering Material	Heat Loss (BTU/sq.ft/hr)
Glass (1/4 inch)	1.13
Double layer glass	0.65
Fibreglass reinforced plastic	1.0
Acrylic sheet (3 mm thick)	1.0
Polythene film	1.15
Polythene film (double layer)	0.70
Polyester film	1.05

Source: *Greenhouse Operation* by Nelson, Prentice Hall

Heating systems

There are two main types of heating systems:

1. Centralised heating system

This is normally a boiler or boilers in one location generating steam or hot water which is piped to one or more greenhouse complexes. This is usually the most expensive to install and may be more expensive to operate. There are side benefits though (e.g. steam which is generated can be used to sterilise soil, pots etc). This type of system is only appropriate in large nurseries.

2. Localised heating systems

This uses several individual heaters, normally blowing hot air into the greenhouse. Hot air is often distributed through a plastic tube (or sleeve), 30 — 60 cm diameter which is hung from the roof and has holes cut at calculated intervals for distribution of warm air.

The main types of localised heaters are:

Unit heaters

These consist of three parts:
1. Fuel is burnt in the firebox to provide heat at the bottom of the unit (the fuel could be gas, oil or something else).
2. Heat rises through a set of thin walled metal tubes or pipes, which heat up.
3. Behind the heated tubes is a fan which blows cold

Simple solar collector used for greenhouse heating. Heat energy from the sun is used to heat water in black plastic pipes which are laid inside the greenhouse.

Small portable greenhouse heaters.

air through the pipes out the other side into the house.

Convection heaters

These are cheap to purchase and as such, are frequently used by hobbyists and small commercial growers. They differ from unit heaters in that they do not have a built-in heat exchanger. Fuel of almost any type can be combusted in the firebox (wood, coal, gas, oil, etc). Hot fumes then pass out of an exhaust pipe which can be placed between rows of plants, above the heater, or wherever you wish. The exhaust pipe should be sufficiently long (or outlets placed far enough from plants) to ensure dangerously hot air does not come in contact with the plants.

A metal stovepipe or insulated ducting is ideal, however, polythene tubing can be used as well. A potbelly stove or something similar could be used as a convection heater.

Electric heaters

In some areas electricity is cheap. If you happen to have cheap electricity, an electric heater may be considered. These generally consist of a heating element and a fan which blows air across the heating element and into the glasshouse. This type of heater can cost as little as 2 cents per hour to operate, but in some places as much as 15 cents or more. (Costs calculated for operating a 2000 watt heater which would be sufficient to heat a 3 m × 5 m greenhouse.)

Radiant heaters

Low energy, infra red radiant heaters have become popular in the USA in recent years. Growers report significant savings on fuel costs.

Solar heaters

There are several types of solar heaters which can be used or adapted for use in greenhouse heating. The components of a solar heater are:

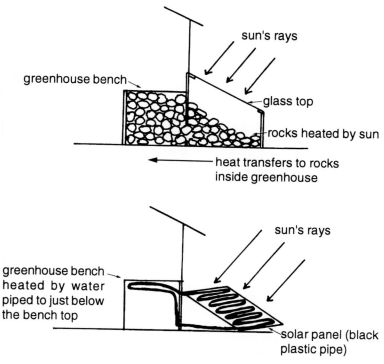

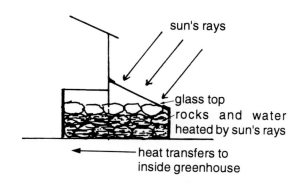

Solar heating

1. Collector These are usually panels heated by direct sunlight. The front is transparent to allow light in; the back is black and insulated to stop energy escaping. Light is converted to heat when it is absorbed by the dark surface.

2. Heat store Water and rocks are two of the most common stores. Water can be passed through the collector and returned to a storage tank of water. Air can pass through the collector and return to the storage tank of rocks.

3. Heat exchanger Pipes or tubes filled with fluid or air pass through the heat store, out through the greenhouse and back to complete the cycle.

A backup heater may be needed to use in conjunction with a solar system.

Composting organic matter

Heat can also be obtained from the composting of organic matter such as fresh animal manures or sawdust. These can be spread as a layer on a section of the floor of the greenhouse. As the materials compost they release a lot of heat. This heat release is irregular and generally only of use for a few months. However it may be a cheap option if a ready supply of organic materials is available, particularly for small structures such as coldframes. It is important that plants are not placed directly on the decomposing materials (unless you are experienced with their use) as they can generate quite high temperatures at times.

Soil and bench warming units

Heating of soil beds, floors or benches is common in many greenhouses. This places the heating zone in close contact with the plants' root zone thereby stimulating root growth. Bottom heaters usually consist of either piped hot water or electric resistance wire which heats up when an electric current passes through it.

Cooling Equipment

During summer months, greenhouses require some type of cooling system. This may range from manually operated vents and shadecloth coverings in simple set-ups to fully-automated cooling fans and ventilators in large commercial ventures.

An evaporative cooling system can be used to lower greenhouse temperatures. This basically

Evaporative cooler on outside of glasshouse wall.

consists of pads on one wall through which water is circulated, and exhaust fans on the opposite wall. Air entering through the pads is cooled and then drawn across the greenhouse to the exhaust fans.

Placement of the pad and fans is important. The most versatile placement of the pad is inside the greenhouse wall, allowing ventilators in that wall to open and close to adjust to weather conditions. Exhaust fans should be at least 5 metres apart from the pad to prevent warm, moist air moving towards an intake pad. When greenhouse walls are less than 4.6 metres apart fans in adjacent walls should be alternated so they do not expel air toward each other.

Ventilation

Use of vents and fans to control temperature and the balance of gases in the greenhouse environment is a very important aspect of the management of any greenhouse. In very large houses, the use of forced air fans becomes more necessary. Air passed through fans can be heated or cooled for additional temperature control. By connecting fans to an electronic thermostat, it is possible to have them switch on and off automatically when ventilation is needed for temperature control. Plants inside a greenhouse should be kept as far away as possible from vents or fan outlets (temperature variations can be more extreme in these positions).

Lighting Equipment

Supplementary lighting is frequently used in greenhouses to assist plant growth. The main types of lights are described below (see also chapter 4):
1. Incandescent (tungsten filament)
These are not ideal for plants. Among other things the quality of light is poor and they create excessive heat. They have a high proportion of red light and this can cause tall, excessively tender plant growth.
2. Fluorescent (e.g. Gro-Lux Fluorescent lamps)
Fluorescent lamps have been useful in propagation areas and with young plants, but are not suitable for plants in the latter stages of production.
3. High intensity discharge (e.g. high pressure mercury or metal halide)
These are the best for plants in the latter stages of production, prior to selling.

Humidifying Equipment

Misting
If intermittent sprays of mist can be applied to the top of cuttings, a temperature differential will develop between the root and leaf zones. If the root zone can be kept warmer than the leaf zone there will be a tendency towards greater growth in the root zone. In other words the warmest part of the plant will grow the fastest.

In addition the increased humidity created by the misting reduces water loss from the cutting.

Misting systems generally have a solenoid valve between the water source and the misting system. The solenoid valves are generally controlled by the following devices:

1. Simple timers which will turn the system on to give a short pulse of water (e.g. 15 seconds) at regular intervals (e.g. 2–5 minutes). Intervals can vary according to season, local conditions, type of plants grown, etc. This type of control is very dependable and can be used to control a number of individual systems at the one time. Their major

disadvantage is that they do not respond to fluctuations in local environmental conditions (e.g. temperature, humidity, light intensity).

2. Sensors such as a pair of carbon electrodes set in an ebonite block (known as an electronic leaf or carbon block sensor) placed under the mist with the cuttings. As the top of the block dries, the current between the sensors is broken. This causes a solenoid valve to open, releasing water into the misting system. The mist then settles on the sensor remaking the electric circuit, which in turn closes the solenoid valve cutting off the water supply.

Another common sensor is the screen balance (or balance arm) control, which has a small stainless steel screen on one end of a balance arm or level to which is attached a mercury switch. When the mist is on water lands on the screen causing it to drop. This trips the mercury switch turning off a solenoid causing it to close. The screen rises as water evaporates, causing the mercury switch to connect, turning on the solenoid and so releasing water. The screen balance should be placed in a position where it will not be affected by wind. Salt deposits and algal growth can affect the balance of the screen, so a regular cleaning program should be carried out. This type of sensor is commonly used in areas where there are considerable fluctuations in conditions during the day.

3. Computer controlled systems that monitor a wide range of environmental variables are increasingly being used in some countries to control misting.

The mist droplet size should ideally be in the vicinity of 50 to 100 micrometres (0.002 – 0.004 inches) diameter. This will be governed by the type of spray nozzle selected.

Fog
Fog systems are a comparatively new development in nursery propagation. They have been found to give extremely good results in striking cuttings. They are used as an alternative to the more traditional method of intermittent misting to provide the cuttings with a humid environment.

The advantage of a fog system is that it creates the humid environment which is necessary to prevent the cuttings from drying out, but eliminates the water droplets which sit on the leaves in mist systems. Fog droplet sizes are less than 20 micrometres and they remain airborne long enough for evaporation to occur so that the water is held

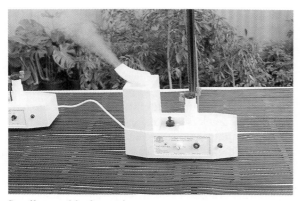

Small portable fog unit.

Greenhouse fog system.

suspended in the air as a vapour. Humidity levels will be in the vicinity of 90–100%.

The absence of free water from the leaves results in:
- reduced fungal problems;
- reduced leaching of leaf nutrients;
- improved aeration of the propagation medium.

Cuttings propagated by this method have given more successful strike rates, and are healthier and faster to develop roots. They are not designed as irrigation systems, so extra watering may be required to prevent the medium from drying out.

Carbon dioxide enrichment

Carbon is an essential plant nutrient and is supplied to the plant in the form of atmospheric carbon dioxide. It is used during daylight hours in the process of photosynthesis, but at times, particularly during winter when greenhouses may be closed to reduce heat loss, carbon dioxide levels may be deficient for plant growth.

To overcome this problem, carbon dioxide is added to the greenhouse during daylight hours. The most common method is through the burning of kerosene, LP gas, or natural gas in special burners inside the greenhouse. Concentrations of 500 to 1500 ppm will help accelerate growth of most crops, although there will be differences in response between varieties.

Alternatively bottled carbon dioxide can be used. This is usually more expensive than using a combustion heater, but has the advantages of not producing heat, which is not always desired, and not producing other gases and/or smoky fumes which can be detrimental to plant growth.

Fertilising and irrigating programs will correspondingly need to be stepped up to match the increased growth rates.

Sheds and Workrooms

Storage Buildings

Buildings used for storage of nursery equipment should be well constructed, and capable of providing suitable protection. The degree of protection will depend on the type of goods being stored. For example, furniture, clothing and electrical tools may require a greater degree of protection than outdoor gardening machinery.

The building should also provide security against burglars, curious children and animals. Cheap storage sheds are available in kit form.

When purchasing or building a storage building consider the following:

• Metal sheds in kit form are usually the cheapest. Some come with each side and roof section already together, and only six or seven pieces to join together so assembly is very easy. Others come in dozens of pieces of framework and panelling, making the assembly job a more tedious process (perhaps a day's work). Metal sheds may rust more readily in seaside areas. Galvanised sheeting is your best option. Metal sheds can be very hot in summer and very cold in winter.

- Brick or timber sheds are better insulated, and are usually longer lasting, but can be expensive to build. Some timbers require more regular protective treatments (e.g. preservative paints) than brick or metal sheds.
- Materials such as fibro-cement or hardiplank are easy to work with and can be a relatively cost effective way of building a shed. They are better insulated than metal sheets.
- Lean-to sheds can be built very easily and cheaply, using an existing wall or fence. Council permits may be required.

Alternatives for roofs and walls
Your choice of material for walls and roofing will make a difference to the way you can use a structure, the amount of maintenance you will have to do, how long the structure will last, how it looks, and how much it costs. Consider the following:

- Insulation
Some materials keep the cold and heat out, others don't.
- Light penetration
If you're going to work or grow plants inside, you will need a certain level of light. This means windows or some sort of light transmitting material such as shadecloth, fibreglass or PVC are preferable for at least part of the roof or wall.
- Ventilation
Air needs to be able to move through the structure to keep it cool inside, and to reduce humidity which can cause mould on walls and roofs or diseases in plants.
- Cost
Cheaper materials may be adequate in the short term but normally have disadvantages in the long term, particularly with regard to maintenance requirements.
- Strength and durability
The type of material and thickness can affect the strength and lifespan. Some timbers will last a lifetime without any treatment, while others need preservatives to protect them against rot. Some metals will corrode. PVC plastics which are UV stabilised will last much longer than non UV stabilised PVC surfacing materials.
- Attaching objects to the wall
Timber walls are simple to attach shelves to, but metal walls may be more difficult, requiring either a pop rivet gun or welding equipment. Some walling materials (e.g. thin metal) may not have the strength to support heavy shelves, other materials are stronger.

Siting Work Buildings and Storage Sheds

You will need to consider the following (while some of these points may appear obvious they are too often neglected):

- Make sure the site has sufficient drainage. This is very important, particularly in areas subject to heavy downpours.
- Good access is important. This includes clear, unobstructed passage into and out of the building, not only for staff and customers but also for moving goods and machinery. Pathways and driveways should ideally be covered with a durable surfacing such as concrete, gravel or pavers to provide a solid, non-slip surface.
- Make sure the building is on a solid base or foundation.
- If earthworks have been carried out, make sure that ground beneath a new building has been well consolidated to prevent later subsidence, and that suitable retaining walls (or alternatives) have been built to prevent erosion or collapse of sloped areas.
- Make sure buildings are well away from trees that have strong root systems that may cause lifting, or large trees that drop a lot of leaves, or even branches.

8 Management

There are many things involved in running a nursery which do not directly relate to horticulture. In fact, nurseries are sometimes managed just as well by people from different industries — as long as they have good general management skills.

Management is all about control, and by exercising control, achieving better results. Good management only occurs when the manager is well informed, hence the first task for any manager is to get to know the organisation they are responsible for.

Managers must appreciate their own role as being the person who controls what happens, *not* the person who actually does the work, unless the nursery is a small operation. A manager who spends a lot of time potting up, weeding plants or talking with customers may find that too little time is being spent running the nursery, and this can result in a loss of control. In a small nursery the manager is often also half of the workforce, so these jobs must be part of his or her routine. A good manager, however, maintains a delicate balance between the various tasks performed each day, and is able to delegate jobs to others in order to help maintain that balance.

Managing People

Recruiting and Interviewing Staff

Finding good staff can be a problem. Many nurseries never go looking for staff, relying instead upon people who just happen to come to them looking for work. This approach ensures that applicants are sufficiently motivated to go looking for work. However, these nurseries may be missing out on people who are so good that they don't have to look for work.

Staff can be sought in the following ways:

1. Approaching horticultural schools
A notice can be placed on a notice board or in a student newsletter, or teachers can be asked for recommendations.

2. Advertising
Appropriate advertising for staff can save time by deterring unsuitable applicants from applying. Advertising in trade magazines will reach people already involved in the trade who are likely to have greater expertise. Advertising in weekend newspapers will reach a much wider variety of people.

3. Employment services
Generally these are good for unskilled labour, but unless they specialise in horticultural staff they are unlikely to be able to put you in touch with skilled staff.

4. Professional associations
Associations are often aware of members who are between jobs or looking to move to a new job. They may also be willing to notify members of employment opportunities through association newsletters.

Interviewing
Interviewing can be time consuming and costly. In large organisations three interviews often take place:

1. Preliminary interview to weed out unsuitable applicants.

2. Employment office interview to select several candidates for the position.

3. Final interview by the prospective supervisor.

In smaller nurseries time can be saved by posting a job application form or questionnaire for applicants to fill out. This can allow many of the applicants to be weeded out without going to the trouble of interviews. Remember that the applicants are associates in the industry and you should try to give them a positive impression of your business. Be courteous and encouraging in your replies, even when you are telling people they are not successful in their application for employment.

Three rules should be followed when interviewing:
1. Keep the appointment time.
2. Avoid interruptions.
3. Make applicants feel at ease.

Job Descriptions

Every applicant should be given a job description, outlining the experience and qualifications needed for the job, the duties and responsibilites involved in the position, and the organisation's conditions of employment.

Examples of Job Descriptions

1. Nursery Manager
Qualifications and Experience Required
The following are essential:
• At least 10 years experience in horticulture, with a minimum of 5 years employment in a production nursery.
• Experience in management supported by positive references from previous employers or business associates.
• The ability to identify a large number of native and non-native trees and shrubs.

The following is preferred:
• Experience in managing a production nursery.
• Membership of professional or trade organisations.
• Formal horticultural qualifications.
• Have attended conferences or seminars in the horticulture industry.
• Marketing experience.

Relationships
• Responsible to the Directors of the nursery.
• In charge of all day-to-day on-site operations.
• Directions to workers to be given via section heads (i.e. forepersons).

Duties
• Prepare work schedules (at least one week in advance in consultation with the Director) for daily work to be carried out in the nursery.
• At the beginning of each day instruct each person in what they should do that day, in accordance with prepared work schedules.
• In person, check what each employee is doing on the site at least twice each day, and correct their work methods/techniques if necessary.
• In conjunction with the Director attend to record keeping, purchase of stock and materials, payment of bills, promotion and marketing.
• Be responsible for ensuring legal requirements in operating the nursery are adhered to, including occupational safety regulations and employee awards.

Conditions
• Position will be reviewed after initial twelve months.
• Two weeks notice to be given in writing to terminate employment.
• Hours 8.30 am to 5 pm, Monday to Friday.
• Four weeks annual leave not to be taken before eleven months have passed.
• Sick pay, etc as required by law.
• Salary negotiable according to experience and qualifications.

Number of Positions
One for one year. Term may be extended.

2. Foreperson Propagator
Relationships
• Responsible to the Nursery Manager.

Duties
• Take charge of all routine work in the potting shed.
• Collect cutting material for propagation.
• Oversee the propagation and potting up of plants under direction from the Nursery Manager.
• Be responsible for monitoring and ordering nursery supplies.
• Maintain propagation records.

Conditions
- Remuneration will be determined in accordance with the hours worked.
- Position will be reviewed after initial twelve months.
- Two weeks notice to be given in writing to terminate employment.
- Hours 8.30 am to 5 pm, Monday to Friday.
- Four weeks annual leave not to be taken before eleven months have passed.
- Sick pay, etc. as required by law.
- Salary negotiable according to experience and qualifications.

Number of Positions
Initially two full-time.

3. Nurseryhand
Relationships
- Take instructions from the Propagator, or from the Manager when the Propagator is absent.

Duties
- Propagate plants.
- Pot up plants.
- Control pests, diseases and weeds.
- Make up and process orders.
- Develop and maintain stock and display gardens.
- Other nursery work as required.

Conditions
- Remuneration will be determined in accordance with hours worked, and will be subject to industry award conditions.
- Position will be reviewed after twelve months.
- Two weeks notice to be given in writing to terminate employment.
- Hours 8.30 am to 5 pm, Monday to Friday.
- Four weeks annual leave not to be taken before eleven months have passed.
- Sick pay, etc. as required by law.

Number of Positions
Initially one full-time or two half-time positions; as production increases the number of nurseryhands will be increased.

4. Administrative/Clerical Officer
Relationships
- Responsible to the Director and Nursery Manager.
- Responsible for all routine office/clerical work.

Duties
- Maintain filing systems.
- Take phone calls.
- Assist with handling correspondence, book keeping, record keeping, taking orders, and general assistance where required.
- Work with and ideally have experience with computerised office systems.

Conditions
- Financial remuneration will be determined in accordance with hours worked.
- Position will be reviewed after initial twelve months.
- Two weeks notice to be given in writing to terminate employment.
- Hours 8.30 am to 5 pm, Monday to Friday.
- Four weeks annual leave not to be taken before eleven months have passed.
- Sick pay, etc. as required by law.

Number of Positions
Initially one full-time.

Defining employees' responsibilities

Responsibilities should be clearly defined, preferably in writing, for all people working in the nursery. A copy of an employee's responsibilities should be given to each employee when they commence work. It is important for a manager to read through the job description point by point with the employee to clarify and reinforce the employee's understanding of what is expected. Managers should evaluate each person's responsibilities on a regular basis, and make adjustments where necessary. The manager should also ask the employee for feedback. The manager might ask the employee every six months to suggest 'anything that can be done' to make his or her work more efficient.

If there are changes to what is expected from an employee, be sure to inform the person concerned when adjustments are made. The employee should be made aware that such adjustments to their job specification can be made, before they commence work.

Motivating Employees

Motivating yourself and others is a key facet to success. We all have certain needs which need to be satisfied: being treated with respect, doing interesting work, working in good conditions and receiving fair pay. These are all motivational factors.

Training Staff

Staff training is an ongoing and necessary aspect of any nursery. In some situations staff training is a legal necessity. In Australia medium to large nurseries are required to spend a percentage of staff wages on training. In other situations, training becomes necessary because new tools, equipment, materials, products or procedures are introduced into the workplace. Many nurseries deal with such changes by simply 'quickly telling their staff' and assuming they will remember. This approach is rarely successful so a more serious approach is necessary if changes are to be adopted and effectively practised.

Training employees makes good sense for many reasons:

• It reduces the time for new employees to reach acceptable levels of performance.
• It saves money, misuse of machinery, waste of materials, etc.
• It provides employees an opportunity to gain new skills.
• It gives employees a feeling of security which helps in the overall development of motivation.

Staff are the greatest asset of any business. Even if you have the best retail site, the best store layout, the best range of products and the most competitive range of products, your business won't work if you have poorly presented, uninformed and uncaring staff.
• Select the best staff and train them better than anyone else.
• Give them every reason to stay in your employment (and give them no reason to leave).
• Make sure your staff know very clearly what is expected of them.
• Always remember that questions from customers can lead to sales. If your staff cannot answer customers' questions in an informative, friendly manner then customers are likely to go elsewhere.
• Good staff will ask the customers lots of questions (e.g. Have you seen this new product?).

Senior staff should set good examples when handling customers. Even if a customer wants to talk to you at an inconvenient moment, it is important to make time to talk to them. If your customers aren't happy then your sales will suffer. If senior staff handle customers well, juniors will tend to handle staff in a similar manner. If some staff do not react to your example, get rid of them quickly before they start to influence others.

Styles of Supervision

Different supervisors will lead their staff in different ways. Often the style is influenced by the personality of the supervisor. Some people need to work harder to be a good supervisor because the best style in the workplace might be different to their natural tendencies. Here are just a few of the different styles which might be adopted by a supervisor:

Domineering These people are the boss, and they expect things done their way, or else! This style has serious flaws and rarely makes for a happy and cooperative group of employees.

Laissez-faire These supervisors just roll along letting things happen rather than making them happen. They may do a reasonable job but they are not usually high achievers.

Democratic This is a cooperative approach where the supervisor makes the ultimate decisions and takes responsibility for those decisions, but constantly seeks the opinions of other staff and lets their opinions have a strong influence on the decisions which are made. This works but risks poor decisions being made if less informed staff have too much influence.

Autocratic but humanistic The supervisor makes the decisions, but welcomes suggestions. The staff do not influence decisions, but their ideas are sought after and always considered.

Giving directives and introducing change

One of the most important tasks for a nursery manager is to tell staff to do something. This sounds easy, but it can be one of the most difficult things to do. Orders are always accepted and followed more readily when given and received in a friendly and positive environment. As such it is essential to always smile and be complimentary when giving orders.

Three different ways of introducing major changes are:

1. Consultation conference
The supervisor calls a meeting with staff to get their views on the proposed change. This does two things: it lets the staff know what changes are proposed, and it lets the supervisor know their likely reaction. There is no bind on the supervisor to follow recommendations or views expressed at the meeting or to convey these thoughts to senior management, although these things may be possible.

2. Participatory decision-making
This is different to the consultation conference, in that decisions reached are binding on the supervisor.

3. Formal consultation schemes
Established by management, this allows employees to make suggestions (e.g. through suggestion boxes).

Giving Orders
Orders can be given as either a spoken or written instruction, or both.

Spoken orders
These can be a command, a request or an implied order. It is important to be clear which of these it is. Vague orders can cause serious problems in the workplace.

Written orders
If the order is important and there is any doubt about the employee's likelihood of carrying it out, it is best reinforced in writing.

Types of written orders include:
• Routine internal order on a prescribed form (e.g. requesting supply of materials or tools from one department to another).
• Special orders which are put in writing because a record of the order is required, or because the supervisor is separated from the worker (e.g. a sales manager may be in a different city to the sales representative he or she is ordering).
• Complex orders — if the job is very complicated, a written order may be required to be communicated properly.

Orders and instructions
Orders and instructions are different things. An order tells the worker what to do (e.g. 'Let Mr Brown know the meeting is off'). An instruction tells the worker what to do and how to do it (e.g. 'Telephone Mr Brown now and tell him the meeting is off').

Procedure for giving detailed orders
The following steps are a useful procedure when giving important or detailed orders:
1. Initial approach.
2. State the job and its objective.
3. Check existing knowledge the worker has regarding the task to be carried out.
4. Tell the employee the importance of the job.
5. Give additional instruction in stages.
6. Stress key points.
7. Have the job explained back to you by the employee.
8. Indicate the worker's level of personal responsibility.
9. Encourage questions.

Procedure for dealing with orders not correctly carried out
1. Ask if the worker does understand the order.
2. Ask the worker why the order was not/cannot be carried out.
3. Ask the worker if he/she realises the importance of the order.
4. Go over instructions fully again.
5. Ask the worker to explain the job fully before doing it.
6. State again the personal responsibility of the worker.
7. Allow questions.

Safety and Illness at Work

Accidents do happen but can be prevented by making sure that:
• the job being done and all surrounds are safe;
• you educate your employees to carry out safe work practices;
• safety rules are enforced.

Accidents occur in four major situations:
1. Wherever materials are handled.
2. Around machines (every type, even computers).
3. Wherever people walk.
4. Wherever hand tools are used.

A supervisor should stress safety at all times because it's his or her problem when an accident occurs.

The Significance of Illness
Sickness or injuries can result in the following:
• Monetary loss to the worker.

- Suffering and stress for the worker and his or her family.
- Loss of production.
- Cost of repairs to equipment damaged by accidents.
- Loss of material spoilt in injury.
- Cost in money and time to train replacement staff.
- In case of repeated accidents, other employees may exhibit unwillingness to do that particular job.
- Accidents which result in damage or injury to non-company people or property can result in bad publicity and high compensation payments.
- Employees who are not in peak health don't work effectively.
- Employees who are stressed, suffer from tension or nervous disorders can be less productive, and cause tension and stress amongst their workmates.

Productivity

A nursery can be thought of as being like a machine where you put things in (soil, plant material, labour and money) and at the other end you take things out (plants and profit). Productivity is the relationship between the inputs and outputs. A nursery is considered more productive when maximum outputs can be achieved with minimum inputs.

Productivity is most commonly measured in dollar terms as a productivity ratio, e.g.

Total productivity = Total output / total input, or

Total productivity = Number of dollars received from plant sales / number of dollars it cost to produce the plants

An indication of productivity levels can be deduced by monitoring specific aspects of daily work such as:
- The number of cuttings taken per day, or the number of plants potted per day by each employee.
- The total value of sales achieved by each salesperson.
- The percentage strike rate of cuttings taken.

Some nurseries keep records of performance factors such as these and encourage greater productivity by giving a bonus or some other benefit to the best performing employee each week or month, or to any worker who achieves a set target (e.g. number of cuttings done per hour averaged over a month).

Costs must continually be watched for changes which might affect overall productivity. Simple things such as changes in the personal life of an employee, increased charges from suppliers, deterioration of equipment, or a change in taxation can have a significant but initially unnoticed effect on productivity. Such changes must be detected and countered quickly, whether by increasing product prices or some other management decision.

Work Scheduling

Planning a work schedule should involve four steps:
Step 1. Define objectives, goals, and tasks to be achieved.
Step 2. Put forward several alternative courses of action.
Step 3. Decide which of the alternative courses of action will give the best result.
Step 4. Put the chosen plan into action.

A worksheet such as the one below can be used to compare alternative courses of action and help with making a decision.

Worksheet for Planning a Work Schedule

Task	Alt. 1	Alt. 2	Alt. 3
Materials and equipment			
What is needed?			
Why that much?			
Would others do?			
Machines and workplaces			
Where must work be done?			
Why there?			
Anywhere else?			
Sequence of work tasks			
When must job be done?			
Why then?			
Any alternatives?			
Method of work			
How should tasks be done?			
Why that way?			
Any alternatives?			
Number and type of employees			
Who should do the job?			
Why them?			
Who else?			

When developing a work schedule consideration should be given to the following:

Interrelated work

Many jobs are interrelated, so planning schedules should consider the effects on other tasks. For example, extra plants can be propagated during wet weather, but there is no value in producing more if the money and labour are not available to maintain and pot up plants later on.

Area of discretion

Employees must know terms, policies and limitations set down by management. For example, if there are strict safety procedures these must be accounted for when allocating time and resources to a certain job.

Routines

Where possible all routine tasks should have set procedures. Different staff can then be allocated certain times to carry out tasks.

Commitment

Courses of action must be consistent with current and future commitments. Resources cannot be used if they have already been allocated.

Cost-benefit

Generally speaking, the least costly course of action is preferred (given that the benefit from each alternative being considered would be the same). If one course returns greater benefit than the others, that is to be preferred.

Credibility

The course of action selected must be acceptable to both your superiors and the workers you are in charge of. If a course of action lacks credibility it should be discarded.

Uncertainty

There should be minimum risk in any course of action which is selected. If there are things which you cannot be sure about (e.g. whether materials will be available on time), then that alternative should be discarded.

Organising the workplace

Like it or not, every manager has to organise his or her workplace. It may involve organising one department or the entire business. A nursery may be reorganised because of change or expansion of the premises, or it may be done in an effort to improve efficiency. We organise to develop good work habits. When organising the workplace the manager must:

- take a realistic look at the future;
- try to accurately forecast problems;
- determine alternative strategies to these problems;
- evaluate available resources.

Whenever reorganising anything (e.g. a work area, office furniture, workshop, stores, etc), the following should be considered:

- Who and what might be affected by reorganising. Staff may resent changes if they are not consulted or made to feel reassured.
- Write down a list of the operations within a section being reorganised (e.g. potting up, propagation, order-taking).
- What physical movement of people, equipment or materials is involved? Find the most convenient and money-saving way of doing this without disrupting work. It may be necessary to do the reorganising on the weekend or after hours.
- Are delays to work likely? If something is stopped or delayed this will be costly, so choose the most effective time to do the reorganising.
- Will anything need to be stored and if so where? For example, records which are not current, or equipment no longer or temporarily not needed.
- An inspection should be made of everything before and after reorganising (e.g. if items are being moved a distance, an inspection checklist can help ensure items are not lost between locations).
- Analyse the reorganisation afterwards. Has the reorganising been successful? Has it saved time and money?

Managing Money

Calculating Costs in a Nursery

At all times, the nursery manager must have a firm control over what it is costing to operate the business.

Costs involved in operating a nursery can be broken down into the following:

1. Land

If this is owned, it still cost something to buy and it could have been leased to someone else to provide a direct income. A cost should always be included for provision of land.

2. Labour

Even if it is you and your family doing the work, you are forgoing the opportunity of earning money elsewhere. Every hour of work put into a nursery should be accounted for, otherwise you will have no real understanding of the business's profitability/efficiency.

Work efficiencies are extremely important. For example, you should consider how many pots can be potted in one hour, or how many cuttings can be done in a day. These types of figures can vary by factors of 100% or more from nursery to nursery. It is important to budget on realistic standards which you, and your workers, are able to achieve, and then closely monitor those standards.

3. Capital

If capital is invested in a nursery, then you are forgoing interest which this capital would attract if invested in some other way.

Any capital borrowed must be paid back with interest. Interest payments must be included in any costing.

Borrowers should keep the following in mind:

• The loan should be for things which will improve the profits or efficiencies of operation. Do not borrow to simply build better working conditions such as a lunchroom or carpark for staff. These should only be developed out of profits which have already been earned.
• Be sure that interest and capital repayments can be met while still maintaining reasonable levels of liquidity.
• Pay back over no more, preferably less, than the period which your newly purchased asset will operate for.

4. Equipment

A nursery can operate with basic equipment such as a spray unit, hoses and moveable sprinklers, a few pairs of secateurs, a work bench, wheelbarrow, etc. On the other hand, purchase of more sophisticated equipment such as potting machinery, computers or automatic irrigation might improve overall profitability by increasing the rate of growth of plants, increasing the quality of your product, decreasing the cost of labour, etc.

The scale of operation will affect the profitability of adding sophisticated equipment to an operation (e.g. a small nursery might be wasting money buying an expensive potting machine because it is only used occasionally).

5. Materials

Soil, fertiliser, growth hormones, plant labels, pots, etc. are all needed to operate a nursery. You can use cheap products of poor quality, or expensive products which might be of better quality. Your selection of materials will affect your plants (their quality and saleability), as well as the cost involved in production.

Example of estimating the cost of cutting production

Cuttings grown 200 to a tray with bottom heat and mist:

1. Materials used   *Cost per tray ($)*
  Plastic tray   . . . . . .
  Propagating mix   . . . . . .
  Label   . . . . . .
  Rooting hormone   . . . . . .
  Cutting material (if stock plants or
  cuttings need to be purchased)   . . . . . .
  Other chemicals (e.g. drench for
  control of disease)   . . . . . .

2. Labour
  Collecting and preparing cuttings   . . . . . .
  Filling trays   . . . . . .
  Inserting cuttings   . . . . . .
  Chemical drenching of tray   . . . . . .
  Placing in propagating area   . . . . . .

3. Operating costs
  Energy cost for running propagating
  area   . . . . . .
  Cost for total area divided by number
  of trays in that area   . . . . . .

The total cost of producing a tray needs to be multiplied by the % strike rate and divided by the number of cuttings to obtain the cost of producing each rooted cutting.

Cash Flow

The availability of cash varies from time to time throughout the year. If plants are mainly sold in spring, then cash will be available in spring from those sales; however, during winter when sales might be minimal, you might be spending a lot on wages but taking in very little. You need to plan ahead for those periods when cash is going to be short, and put aside money in the good times, to carry your operation in the bad times. A cash flow chart can easily be produced by listing the months and writing in when cash is going out and coming in (see below).

Cash flow chart for a wholesale nursery in a temperate climate

	Expenditure	Income
January		Low sales
February	Pots and soil	Low-medium sales
	Seasonal labour-cuttings	
March	Pay income tax	Medium (autumn) sales
	Casual labour	
April		Medium (autumn) sales
May		Low-medium sales
June		Low sales
July		Low-medium sales
August	Casual labour	Medium sales
September	Pots and soil Casual labour	Medium sales
October	Casual labour	High (spring) sales
November	Casual labour	High (spring) sales
December		Medium sales

Note: The above chart is only partially filled in, and of course your situation will be different, however the concept remains the same. Preparation of a cash flow chart will help you gain a broad picture of your cash flow throughout the year.

Financial Statements

There are two main financial statements: the Balance Sheet and the Profit and Loss Statement. These give the financial situation of a nursery at a set period of time.

Monthly financial statements are usually the best records to determine how well the nursery is going. The monthly statements will show the cash flow situation. Early in a nursery's development it may be necessary to do cash flow statements weekly.

Simple examples of these two types of statements are set out below. Many nurseries prepare these and other financial statements and records using simple computerised accounting packages. For advice on which of these would suit your needs consult your accountant or firms selling computer software.

Example of the Balance Sheet

Balance sheet of GreenPlant Wholesale Nursery to June 30 1994

Liabilities and Proprietorship		Assets	
Current liabilities		**Current Assets**	
Bank overdraft	$10,000	Cash and bank accounts	$2,386.27
Accounts payable	$ 3,560	Stock inventory	$29,565.00
Long-term liabilities		**Fixed Assets**	
Debentures	$20,000	Equipment	$42,500.00
Mortgage	$25,000	Property	$155,000.00
Proprietorship			
Owner's capital	$170,089.27		
Total	$229,451.27		$229,451.27

Example of the Profit and Loss Statement

Profit and Loss Statement for GreenPlant Wholesale Nursery from 1/7/93–30/6/94

Net sales	$65,000
Less cost of producing plants:	
Materials	
Labour	
Depreciation charges	
Miscellaneous operating costs	
Total production cost	$22,000
Add: Opening inventory	$30,165
Deduct: Closing inventory	$29,565
Equals: Cost to produce plants sold	$22,600
Gross profit	$42,400
Less Marketing and administration costs	$6400
Less taxes, rates, interest	$9300
Net profit	$26,700

The Cash Book

The cash book is simply a book into which you write all financial transactions. Money which is received is placed on the right hand column under credit (Cr); money spent is placed under the left hand side column under debit (Dr).

Example of the cash book

Date	Item	Dr	Cr
24/2/94	Postage — general	$24.70	
24/2/94	Order — school		$158.00
24/2/94	Petrol — delivery van	$30.00	
25/2/94	Rent — for February	$855.00	
25/2/94	Cash sale		$395.00

Records

Accurate records must be kept on every aspect of a nursery's operation. These are often necessary for taxation purposes, but are also an invaluable management tool allowing control of daily operations and necessary analysis of trends for planning future operations. You should keep records of what you are spending, the monies which are coming in, the plants which are in stock and their current value.

Filing Information
Filing involves classification, arrangement and storage of records. Information which is filed can include:
- Statistical data
- Reports of former events
- Product information (including price lists)
- Employee records
- Enquiries
- Accounts

Information can be filed a number of different ways including:
- Card files
- Filing cabinets
- Computer files
- Microfilm

Filing Procedures
The three main ways of organising information are:
1. Alphabetically
There is a limit to the number of files or the amount of information stored (because there are a limited number of letters to file under). This system is easily used by untrained staff. The disadvantage is that information which is related can be located in different parts of the files.
2. Numerically
This system overcomes problem of having related information in separate sections. Also, the limitation imposed by the restricted number of letters is avoided. The system takes a little longer for a new person to learn.
3. An alphabetical-numerical system
This system involves using either guide cards (in a card file), or a reference book with subjects arranged in alphabetical order. The card file or book tells you where to look in the file to find certain information (which is filed under a numerically arranged system).

Active and inactive records
There are two types of files:
1. Ones which concern work which is current. These must be accessible.
2. Files which concern things which are no longer relevant to daily work. They need not be so accessible; but they should be kept for a certain period. They may need to be kept for legal reasons (certain records are required to be kept by law); or they may be needed in the future (e.g. employees who have left the company may some time later make claims on the company with respect to accidents or other matters which arose during their term of employment).

Stock control

Stock control is an important part of managing any nursery. Records of current stock are used to assist in designing marketing programs and to keep track of how much capital is tied up in stock.

Keeping Records in Propagation
The average propagator rarely keeps detailed records of what and how they propagate. Propagation records provide a valuable source of information for a variety of reasons, including the following:

- Long-term records allow comparison of different types of seed and cutting treatments. For example, you can assess which type of germination treatment gives the best long-term germination rate for a particular seed type, or which hormone concentration or combination of hormones gives the best strike rate for different types of cuttings.

- The records enable you to assess which propagators in the nursery produce the best results. Does one propagator get consistently good results in comparison to another for the same propagation tasks? This can be very valuable economically and also as a guide for staff training programs.

• You may also be able to assess which spot or location in your propagating area gives the best result in terms of germination or strike rates. This can be helpful when choosing where to place particular plants in your propagating area and in trying to determine the environmental conditions that give the best results.

• Keeping records of the source of your propagating material can be very useful in determining if different sources of material for a particular plant give different results.

• Records will help you to determine which plants strike more quickly than others, or which plants give consistent results. This can be very important when deciding which plants to grow (in terms of economic return), and also where to place your plants in the propagating area (e.g. to aid production schedules you might place all the fast-growing plants together).

• Timing of propagation can often be determined from long-term records. (e.g. if a particular plant consistently gets its best propagation results at a particular time of year and does poorly at other times you can arrange your propagation schedules accordingly).

What To Record
Records can be kept in a card file system, a record book or ledger style arrangement, or on a computer based system.

The first step is to keep a daily record of production. This simply records the type of plants propagated, how many propagated, the propagation method, and the date and name of the propagator/s. The simple table below gives an example of how to draw up a daily record form.

Daily Propagation Record Sheet

Plant name	Quantity	Propagation method	Propaga-tor/s	Date
. . . .	. . . .	. . . .	. . . .	. . . . .

The next step is to produce a record for each particular crop. An example of what to record is shown below:

Botanical name . . . .

Common name . . . .

Propagated/sown (date) . . . .

Rooted/breaking (date) . . . .

Method . . . .

Size (for cuttings) . . . .

Medium . . . .

Bottom heat . . . .

Treatments . . . .

No. or grams of seed/cuttings per tray . . . .

Area to be placed . . . .

Date/s potted up . . . .

No. potted up . . . .

Source of prop. material . . . .

Date obtained . . . .

Propagator/s . . . .

Results (e.g. % rooted) . . . .

Comments (e.g. attacked by insects) . . . .

At a later date, the results from these cards can be consolidated into a single set of records and analysed.

Managing the Office

Office Equipment

An enormous range of office equipment is available. The nurseryperson should choose carefully what he or she uses though. It is easy to buy unnecessary gadgets, or equipment which really does not suit.

Office equipment includes such things as desks, chairs, pinboards, partitions, file trays, filing cabinets, card files, bookshelves, photocopiers, printing or duplicating equipment, typewriters, computers, word processors and collating machines.

The new nursery should equip slowly (not only

because of cost considerations, but also because it is easier to decide what you really need after you have been operating for a while). Established business should only change equipment after careful consideration of all the alternatives. Some considerations might be:

• Can you do the same job with something cheaper? (Expensive desks and chairs might look better but in a functional office which is rarely visited by people outside of the business, who is going to care?)
• Is the equipment likely to become obsolete?
• Will you get full use from the equipment? (Will it be used one hour a fortnight and simply take up space the rest of the time?)
• What is the service and parts supply like? (A cheap computer printer is useless if you cannot get ribbons for it. A photocopier must be from a company which has an excellent service record. This consideration cannot be overemphasised!)
• How long will the equipment last? Is it durable and well built?
• Is the equipment ergonomically sound? (Ergonomics is concerned with the relationship between the human body and the equipment it interacts with. For instance, an ergonomically designed chair will cause less strain on the back).
• Is the equipment economical? (What does it cost in cleaning, servicing or other maintenance costs? What labour costs are involved in using the equipment? How comfortable or easy is it for staff to use?)

Office equipment can be leased or purchased. You should only ever lease over the period which the item concerned is being depreciated over. For example, if you have a photocopier and are depreciating it 20% per year, you should lease over no more than 55 years.

Telephone

The way in which you answer a telephone and speak to people is very important to the image of your business. For many of your customers and clients, the first time they have contact with you will be when they phone you. (As they say, first impressions are lasting ones.)

When answering the phone, you should simply say either:
• Your business name, e.g. 'GreenPlant Nursery', or
• Hello, Good day or some similar greeting,

followed by your business name, e.g. 'Good morning; GreenPlant Nursery'.

Some businesses might just state the name of the proprietor of the business, if the business is known by that name. In larger organisations, extensions on a telephone are usually answered by stating the name of the person or department.

Throughout a phone discussion it is important to cultivate a voice tone which is lively and interesting. Do not speak in a monotone. The tone of your voice should go up and down, varying in pitch and speed (but in a subtle way). A friendly, happy voice on the phone is a great asset in any business.

End the phone discussion in a friendly way. A cheerful goodbye is acceptable. In some situations, it may be even better to say 'Have a nice day', or 'Hope to hear from you again soon'.

Computers In the Nursery

by David Mason, Computer Consultant

Since the early 1980s, personal computers have been used by small businesses and increasingly in nurseries to make life easier. They take the repetitiveness out of searching through files for a company's phone number and speed the calculation of numbers in a spread sheet. They allow a company to create its own newsletter, signs or banners, to control payroll runs, and generally to become more efficient.

Apart from general office tasks such as these, computers can have a host of additional uses in a nursery, ranging from controlling aspects of the environment in which plants grow (e.g. switching on and off heaters, coolers and irrigation systems), to bar coding of plant stock to aid stock control, and as an information data base to advise on technical problems as they arise. Some functions are not readily available because the software (i.e. computer programs) is either too expensive or hasn't been written. However, in the near future these things will become available and the applications for using a computer in nursery management will continue to increase.

Software and Hardware
Hardware is a term used to refer to the machinery which makes up a computer system. It is the tangible

parts of a computer: the things which you see and touch (the screen, the keyboard, the case, the electronic circuits, etc).

Software is the intangible part of a computer: the programs, or if you like, the instructions which people have put into and stored in the computer. A computer is useless without software.

A piece of software is a program that allows you to interact with a computer, such as a game or word processor. A major problem in the past has been incompatibility between programs. All software data files are written in special code that may only be read by its creator, thus eliminating the ability to upgrade your system to a different software package. The situation is changing with an increasing trend towards standardisation and cross-compatibility. Unfortunately, these changes will make some software redundant.

Choose carefully, by looking for software that has a well established name. Look in computer magazines, or ask a computer dealer about commonly used software packages.

Types of software

1. System software   This is the operating system for your computer, like the desk you do your work on. There are many different types of operating systems, each with its own advantages and disadvantages. The most common system is DOS (disk operating system).

2. Utility software   These are software 'tools' that help manage, repair and generally look after your PC. These may be programs such as hard disk repairers, file backup programs or undelete utilities.

3. Application software   This is the software the user most commonly operates. It consists of programs such as word processors, databases, spreadsheets, games and desktop publishers.

Computer Specifications

New computer users are often bewildered by confusing techno-jargon such as RAM, ROM and hard disk. To put it simply, a computer is made up of many components. The first and most important part is the motherboard. This is the control centre for the computer that all the other components plug into. On this board of microscopic electronic components resides the CPU (Central Processing Unit), or the brain of the computer. The majority

of instructions are controlled by this, as it makes sure that all of the peripherals work in perfect synchronisation.

The 'ports' or plugs on a computer are attached to devices such as a monitor (the display screen), keyboard (allowing user to type instructions to the PC), mouse (a directional input device), and printer (for hard-copy output).

Also commonly found inside a computer box are floppy disk drives and/or hard disks. Floppy disk drives come in two sizes: 3.5" (the industry standard) and the older 5.25" drives. Floppy disks are like small magnetic plates that store data (usually less than 2 million characters). The older 5.25" disks come in a protective case, whilst the higher capacity 3.5" come in a much sturdier plastic case with metal shutters to protect the disk inside.

Hard disks are huge built-in disks that can store billions of characters of data. They are also a lot faster to access the data than floppy disks. They are not removable.

Applications

Word Processing

Word processing does the same job as a typewriter, except that the writer can change the text before printing a paper copy. It has the added benefit that the text can be saved or stored away on the computer, then recalled (altered if need be) and printed again, whenever required.

Good word processing software can be used for a wide range of purposes in the nursery, including writing business letters and printing posters or advertising brochures. For example, a retail nursery could write, store and print off information sheets for customers as required; a wholesaler could develop and print catalogues and price lists.

Spreadsheets

Spreadsheets are an excellent way of keeping track of expenses, budgets, statistics, etc. A spreadsheet is a large table that consists of cells that contain certain data. You can make these cells relative to each other by using formulas. For example, you might have a spreadsheet set out like the following example:

	1	2	3	4
A		Car 1	Car 2	Car 3
B	January	$100	$ 50	$100
C	February	$110	$1000	$100
D	March	$ 90	$ 90	$200
E	April	$200	$ 70	$100
F	May	$500	$ 500	$ 50
G	June	$700	$ 20	$900
H				
I	Total			

The cells are named by their coordinates on the spreadsheet (e.g. January is in cell B1 and Car 2 is in cell A3). If you wanted a formula to add all of the values for one car and place the value next to Total, you would move to cell I2 and type '=sum(B2:G2)'. This tells the computer to add all the values from B2 to G2. This also means that if any values are changed for Car 1, the change will be reflected in the Total.

Another advantage with spreadsheets is the ability to embed or put graphs into the sheet that relates to the data. These are also updated in the same way as formulas.

Databases

Databases are probably the most commonly used computer program. They are an electronic substitute for a card file system. Databases enable you to keep and print off mail-lists, keep records of suppliers and customers, and to keep track of stock. You are able to sort through large amounts of data much faster when it is stored on computer.

Computerised Environmental Control

The environment around plants can be controlled with computers. There are three parts to such a system:

1. Sensors: These sense changes in the environment such as a drop in temperature, dryness in the air or soil, lack of ventilation, lack of light or an imbalance in the gases in the air.

2. Environmental control equipment: These are things used to correct environmental changes such as heaters, cooling machines, automatic vents, artificial lights, gas injection equipment, etc.

3. Computers: Computers link the sensors to the environmental control equipment and activate or deactivate the equipment when the sensors tell the computer that a predetermined set of conditions have been met.

These systems may be relatively simple or extremely complex, dealing with only one aspect of the environment such as water, or many factors. Computer systems and programs designed specifically for environmental control are available, but shop around as this is still a developing field and some systems may not yet be tried and proven.

Bar Coding in the Nursery

by Brian Collins, D4 Data

Bar codes are a small block made up of series of lines of varying width and distances apart. Each bar code can be made uniquely different to all others. Sensors can be used to distinguish between different bar codes and match these to different batches of information which are put into a computer. The user can readily alter this information.

The system of bar coding common in shops has application in the retail nursery. These systems eliminate the need for staff to remember prices. With long queues at registers in peak seasons (e.g. early spring), the availability of bar coded plants can help speed up customer service.

Some nursery items such as chemicals and fertilisers come to the retailer with a bar code already on the packaging. Similarly, bar codes can be either printed on plant labels or stuck to a plant pot. Alterations to prices are then a simple change to the computer scanner memory or using a different label.

The benefits of bar code labels are not restricted to retailers. They can be used effectively by growers within their own operations. Bar code labels may be used in conjunction with handheld data entry terminals to prepare invoices, collect and update production records, and accelerate and improve accuracy in stocktaking.

Planning

A business plan is essential for any commercial nursery because it forecasts the nursery's viability and can assist with obtaining bank loans. A business plan should take into account the nursery's desired productivity and systematically set out what should be done to reach that goal.

There are many different ways of setting out a business plan. Some are very detailed, others less so. Some present a plan for only one year, and others for many years.

The following example shows just one way of setting out a business plan. This is a serious and viable plan but given the uniqueness of every situation it would need to be carefully adapted to suit the reader's own circumstances.

Example of a nursery development business plan

Synopsis

GreenPlant Wholesale Nursery is a hypothetical wholesale nursery which is to be set up in a country town, within close proximity to a major city. The nursery is sited on two hectares with the option to expand. Initially three experienced full-time staff will be employed with other staff being employed and trained as required. The long-term plan (after five years of operation) is to develop a retail area and a tourist display garden as an adjunct to the wholesale nursery.

1.0 Introduction

The proposed wholesale nursery will be a relatively simple operation. This is due to the nature of material being produced — mostly varieties easily grown from seed or cuttings. Initially it will require a work building, storage areas, a propagating structure (polyhouse), an additional 2 polyhouses for establishing newly transplanted seedlings and rooted cuttings, and a shadehouse area for growing on and hardening off stock.

Growing media should, at least in the early stages, be purchased from city suppliers. Despite the distance, city suppliers will be able to supply the quality mixes needed to ensure good results. It would be too expensive and complicated to attempt to make mixes on site in the early stages of development.

The basis of production will be the propagation of 'in demand' and standard regular selling varieties in tubes. The principal markets for these plants will be retail and wholesale growing-on nurseries. Other markets might include direct sales to the general public, farmers, parks departments, tourists, and production for specialist retailers in other cities. Some of the plants produced in early years could also be used to develop the nursery (e.g. stock plants, windbreak plantings for the garden area, and native gardens as part of the future tourist development).

The nursery facilities will cover up to two hectares of the property in the early years and will have the capacity to produce at least 100,000 plants in the first year. Within five years, the annual level of production should increase to 500,000 plants. The precise rate of growth will depend to a large extent upon:

1. The effectiveness of marketing strategies.
2. The plant varieties grown.
3. The quality of plants produced.
4. The productivity levels attained by the staff.

2.0 Initial Requirements

Step 1 Before any detailed site planning or construction occurs, it is important that those who will be working on the site should get a firm grasp of what is involved in the daily operations of a nursery.

Step 2 A broad concept plan will developed for the site. This should be drawn up by a consultant skilled in both nursery operations and general landscape design working with the management group. The plan should cover not only the nursery layout and design, but also include the garden, stock plant areas, display garden areas, etc. This plan should not be regarded as inflexible — it will change and evolve as the project develops.

Step 3 The next step is to develop basic nursery facilities. This should take three to four weeks. The nursery staff will be involved in the construction of the nursery. This is very important as a way of familiarising the nursery staff with the facilities and equipment they will be using.

Some initial market research could be undertaken at this time:

1. To establish up-to-date information on what plant species are likely to be in demand in the near future (when the first batches of plants become ready for sale).
2. To investigate specific avenues for selling once the first batches are ready. This may involve placing advertisements and taking advance orders.

Step 4 Sufficient propagating material will be required to commence production. Seed would be purchased or collected in the wild, and plants (to use as a source of cuttings) would be acquired while the construction of basic nursery facilities progresses.

Step 5 Propagation should start as soon as the main nursery facilities have been completed. The first month of operations (including at least two weeks of propagation activity) should be considered a training period. It is extremely important that a skilled, experienced and commercially successful nurseryperson manage this period of the operation.

2.1 Initial Nursery Staffing Levels

It is envisaged that the nursery will initially provide enough work to fully occupy three to four full-time workers, and several casual/part-time staff.

3.0 Production Schedule and Estimated Gross Returns for GreenPlant Wholesale Nursery

The following production schedule provides for the progressive development of the GreenPlant Wholesale Nursery to a production level of approximately 500,000 plants per annum after five years.

Notes: The following notes apply to the figures listed in the production schedule.

[1] This assumes that operations commence in July–August (to coincide with the commencement of peak seed sowing period).

[2] This row of figures is based on one propagator initially working on cuttings 5 days/week and one

Five-year Production Schedule (returns based on 1991 prices)

Year 1

Month[1] (no.)	Cuttings[2] (no.)	Plants to tube up[3]		Plants ready to sell (no.)		Nett return[5] ($)
		Cuttings (no.)	Seed (no.)	Total	80%[4]	
1	5000					
2	10,000	1625	3000			
3	12,000	4875	4000			
4	12,000	7150	5000	4625	3700	2442
5	15,000	7800	5000	8875	7100	4686
6	15,000	8775	5000	12,150	9720	6415
7	15,000	9750	8000	12,800	10,240	6758
8	20,000	9750	8000	13,775	11,020	7273
9	20,000	11,375	8000	17,750	14,200	9372
10	20,000	13,000	8000	17,750	14,200	9372
11	20,000	13,000	8000	19,375	15,500	10,230
12	20,000	13,000	8000	21,000	16,800	12,600
					102,480	$69,148

Year 2

Month	Cuttings	Cuttings	Seed	Total	80%	Nett return
1	20,000	14,000	8000	22,000	17,600	11,616
2	20,000	14,000	10,000	22,000	17,600	11,616
3	20,000	14,000	10,000	22,000	17,600	11,616
4	20,000	14,000	10,000	24,000	19,200	12,672
5	20,000	14,000	10,000	24,000	19,200	12,672
6	20,000	14,000	10,000	24,000	19,200	12,672
7	20,000	14,000	10,000	24,000	19,200	12,672
8	20,000	14,000	10,000	24,000	19,200	12,672
9	20,000	14,000	10,000	24,000	19,200	12,672
10	20,000	14,000	10,000	24,000	19,200	12,672
11	20,000	14,000	10,000	24,000	19,200	12,672
12	20,000	14,000	10,000	24,000	19,200	12,672
					225,600	$148,896

Year 3

1	25,000	13,000	12,000	24,000	19,200	12,672
2	25.000	13,000	12,000	24,000	19,200	12,672
3	25,000	17,500	12,000	25,000	20,000	13,200
4	25,000	17,500	12,000	25,000	20,000	13,200
5	25,000	17,500	12,000	29,500	23,600	15,576
6	25,000	17,500	12,000	29,500	23,600	15,576
7	25,000	17,500	12,000	29,500	23,600	15,576
8	25,000	17,500	12,000	29,500	23,600	15,576
9	25,000	17,500	12,000	29,500	23,600	15,576
10	25,000	17,500	12,000	29,500	23,600	15,576
11	25,000	17,500	12,000	29,500	23,600	15,576
12	25,000	17,500	12,000	29,500	23,600	15,576
					267,200	$176,352

Year 4

1	30,700	21,500	15,000	29,500	25,075	16,550
2	30,700	21,500	15,000	29,500	25,075	16,550
3	33,200	23,250	19,000	36,500	31,025	20,477
4	33,200	23,250	19,000	36,500	31,025	20,477
5	33,200	23,250	19,000	42,250	35,913	23,702
6	33,200	23,250	20,000	42,250	35,913	23,702
7	33,200	23,250	20,000	42,250	35,913	23,702
8	33,200	23,250	20,000	43,250	36,763	24,263
9	33,200	23,250	20,000	43,250	36,763	24,263
10	33,200	23,250	20,000	43,250	36,763	24,263
11	37,150	26,000	22,000	43,250	36,763	24,263
12	37,150	26,000	22,000	43,250	36,763	24,263
					403,754	$266,475

Year 5

1	37,150	26,000	22,000	48,000	40,800	26,928
2	37,150	26,000	22,000	48,000	40,800	26,928
3	37,150	26,000	22,000	48,000	40,800	26,928
4	37,150	26,000	22,000	48,000	40,800	26,928
5	37,150	26,000	22,000	48,000	40,800	26,928
6	37,150	26,000	22,000	48,000	40,800	26,928
7	37,150	26,000	22,000	48,000	40,800	26,928
8	37,150	26,000	22,000	48,000	40,800	26,928
9	40,000	28,000	24,000	48,000	40,800	26,928
10	40,000	28,000	24,000	48,000	40,800	26,928
11	40,000	28,000	24,000	52,000	44,200	29,172
12	40,000	28,000	24,000	52,000	44,200	29,172
					496,400	$327,624

propagator/tuber working on cuttings 2 days/week and seeds 3 days/week, with both staff working an 8 hour/day, 45 weeks/year.

—In 1 year a propagator producing 750 cuttings per day (average number for a relatively unskilled propagator) would produce 170,000 cuttings/year.

—In 1 year the propagator/tuber would produce 67,500 cuttings.

—Total cuttings produced = 237,500/year (average 20,000 per month. This figure will be less in the first year due to periods of training).

[3] This row of figures is based on:

a) an estimated 65% strike rate of cuttings which take six weeks from the time of taking the cuttings to tubing up. This figure will vary considerably according to species, time of year, etc.

b) sufficient seed sown to give this minimum number for tubing.

[4] This row of figures assumes that an average 80% of tubed seedlings and cuttings will survive the potting/hardening up stages.

The estimates for cutting strike rates and the

survival of cuttings and seedlings after tubing are conservative estimates based on survival rates at other tubestock nurseries in the locality.

[5] This row of figures is based on an average return of 66c/plant (prices will vary: cuttings will provide a higher return — about 70c; seedlings — about 60c).

Year 1

Initial production will be comparatively lower than average due to the inexperience of staff, lack of stock material, and periods of staff training. By the end of the first year the propagators should have sufficient expertise to achieve a 70% strike rate for cuttings in subsequent years.

Year 3

By this stage additional polyhouses could be purchased using the returns from the previous year. Production of tubestock will correspondingly increase.

4.0 Initial Costs

There will be four major types of costs associated with the establishment and subsequent operation of the GreenPlant Wholesale Nursery. These are:

1. Capital costs — this will include the initial purchase of land and buildings, propagating structures, vehicles and trailers, etc. Most of the capital costs will occur in the first six months.

2. Operating costs — this will include those products or materials that will be 'used up' in the production of plants (pots, chemicals, potting soils, seed trays, etc.). These costs will expand in line with increased production levels, i.e. as more plants are grown then more potting mix and pots will be required.

This section also includes other operational costs not directly related to plant production including insurance, rates, phone, electricity and office materials.

3. Labour costs — this includes the employees' wages, holiday pay, work care levies, super-annuation, etc.

4. Training costs — this includes the costs of courses undertaken by the staff, attendance at workshops, conferences and seminars, and reference books and manuals.

4.1 Propagating and Growing-on Structures

The nursery will initially require three polyhouses, each comprising approximately 60 square metres of floor space. Additional polyhouses covering approximately 180 square metres of floor space will be required in the third year of production and a further 120 square metres in the fifth year.

A shadehouse area of approximately 150 square metres will be required initially with a further shadehouse area of approximately 150 square metres required in the third year of production and a further 150 square metres in the fifth year. Sufficient undercover work space with benches will be required for the preparation of cuttings and for tubing.

4.2 Nursery Equipment and Consumable Materials

Assuming there is no need to mix and sterilise growing media, the equipment required for the nursery will include a range of propagating tools (knives, secateurs, dibbles, etc.), material handling equipment (trolleys, wheelbarrows, shovels, etc.), and other items such as backpack sprayers, protective clothing and other safety equipment.

Consumable materials include chemicals, hormone preparations, fertilisers, growing media, trays, pots, tubes and labels. An indication of the types, quantities and approximate costs of both non-consumable and consumable materials required to produce the target production for the first five years of operations is listed in Table 4.3.

4.3 Summary of Major Costs

Table 4.3 (page 108) includes a listing of facilities, equipment, and services required for the establishment and operation of the GreenPlant nursery, and the associated costs (excluding labour and training costs).

5.0 Projected Nursery Income

Some assumptions are made in the following tables and the figures are largely best estimates. Assessments of costs and profits will depend on productivity, sales and labour costs.

Table 5.1 GreenPlant Wholesale Nursery Projected Income (in 1991 dollars)

Table 5.1 is based on Capital Costs written off in the year purchased, but this is not usual. Capital items are depreciated over a period of time, with the rate of depreciation depending on the item. An accumulative figure over the period is shown in the brackets.

Table 4.3 Summary of Major Costs — excluding labour and training (figures in 1991 dollars)

Year	1	2	3	4	5
Capital Costs					
Property purchase*	140,000				
Grading site and preparing garden beds	700				
Drainage pipes	2000				
Vehicle	23,000			23000	
Trailer	1500				1500
Propagation houses	1700 x 1		1700 x 1		
Polyhouses	1700 x 2		1700 x 2	1700 x 2	
Irrigation equipment	5000		5000		3000
Surfacing material					
Weed mat	210		210		140
Gravel (no fines)	2000			2000	1500
Hotbeds	3000		3000		3000
Shadehouse	1000		1000		1000
Stock plants	2000	500	500	1000	1000
Hand tools	1200	500	500	500	500
Nursery barrows/trolleys	250 x 3		250 x 2		250 x 2
Computer/printer	2000				2000
Potting and work benches	500			800	
Office equipment	2000		1500	1500	2000
Office furniture	1000			1000	
Total	$192,960	$1000	$17,310	$33,200	$16,140
Operating Costs					
Consumables					
Fertilisers	1900	4200	5100	7600	9500
Pesticides	150	200	270	370	500
Hormones	100	200	300	400	500
Disinfectant	75	100	150	200	250
Spray equipment	500	100		500	200
Trays	3600	7400	8200	13,200	17,000
Pots	5200	12,000	13,500	21,000	25,000
Soils	2200	4500	5600	8200	10,400
Petrol	5000	6500	7500	12,000	15,000
Office stationery	500	300	300	400	400
Plant labels	1500	2300	2700	4000	5000
Total Consumables	20,725	37,800	44,120	67,870	83,750
Other Costs					
Rates	2500	2500	2500	2500	2500
Insurance					
Car	600	600	600	1200	1200
Building	700	700	700	700	700
Public Liability	1000	1000	1000	1000	1000
Phone	500	700	900	1100	1200
Power	2000	2000	3000	3000	4000
Water	1800	2000	2500	3200	4200
Advertising/marketing	5000	3000	3000	5000	5000
Total Other Costs	14,100	12,500	14,200	17,700	19,800
Total Operating Costs	34,825	50,300	58,320	85,570	103,550

*This is based on the purchase of a suitable property with buildings and sheds already existing, or the purchase of a property and subsequent construction of suitable facilities.

Table 5.1 Projected income for Green Plant Wholesale Nursery (figures in 1991 dollars)

Capital costs ($) (a)	Operating costs ($) (b)	Labour costs ($) (c)	Total costs ($) (d) = (b) + (c)	Sales ($) (e)	Nett Profit/Loss ($) (f) = (e) − (d)
Year 1					
192,960	34,825	76,472	304,257	69,148	235,109 loss
Year 2					
1000	50,300	76,472	127,772	148,896	21,124 profit (213,985 loss)
Year 3					
17,310	58,320	76,472	152,102	176,352	24,250 profit (189,735 loss)
Year 4					
33,200	85,570	125,972	244,742	266,475	21,733 profit (168,002 loss)
Year 5					
16,140	103,550	125,972	245,662	327,624	81,962 profit (86,040 loss)

The table below shows the effect on profit and loss when capital costs are not included. An accumulative figure over the period is shown in the brackets.

Capital costs ($) (a)	Operating costs ($) (b)	Labour costs ($) (c)	Total costs ($) (d) = (b) + (c)	Sales ($) (e)	Nett Profit/Loss ($) (f) = (e) − d)
Year 1					
192,960	34,825	76,472	111,297	69,148	42,149 loss
Year 2					
1000	50,300	76,472	126,772	148,896	22,124 profit (20,025 loss)
Year 3					
17,310	58,320	76,472	134,792	176,352	41,560 profit (21,535 profit)
Year 4					
33,200	85,570	125,972	211,542	266,475	54,933 profit (76,468 profit)
Year 5					
16,140	103,550	125,972	229,522	327,624	98,102 profit (174,570 profit)

5.1 Potential Profit Increases

There is potential to increase the profit rate as listed above. If a high level of direct retail sales can be achieved, then retail prices can be charged which will yield higher returns per plant. For example, a tubestock seedling that might wholesale for 65 cents could be sold for up to $1 retail, and as the plant is being sold directly from the nursery there would be no transport costs involved.

It may also be worthwhile considering some limited production of larger container-grown plants for direct retail sales. This could also be a useful way to utilise any unsold tubestock. Instead of throwing the plants away or using them for on-site plantings, the tubestock could be potted up, for example into a 12 cm pot. A plant in this size pot may cost $1.50 to $2.00 to produce and have a wholesale price of $2.50, but retail between $3.50

and \$4.00. Thus even retail sales of 2000 x 12 cm pots per annum could add as much as \$4000 to the total annual gross profit.

Practical Exercise

1. Consider the formula:
   Cost of Production + profit = Sales price
2. Plan the establishment of a new wholesale nursery which is to produce trees and shrubs in 125 mm plastic pots.
3. Set a sales price for plants to be produced (be realistic). You may find it helpful to look at the sales price of 125 mm pots in local nurseries.
   Sales price = ...
4. Set a profit figure for the formula (probably 20 or 30% of sales price, depending on the scale of production).
   Profit = ...
5. Calculate what your cost of production should be.
   Cost of production (per plant) = ...
6. On the basis of the cost of production you have set, prepare a budget for the first year's operation of this new nursery. Fill in costs below:

Budget

Number of plants to be produced in the first year ......

Number of plants to be thrown away (because they die, become diseased, get too woody, etc) ......

Number of plants sold in first year .....

Money generated through sales (income) .....

Cost of Production

Property and services	\$ ....
Materials	\$ ....
Pots	\$ ....
Soil	\$ ....
Fertiliser	\$ ....
Other chemicals	\$ ....
Stationery	\$ ....
Labour	\$ ....
Advertising/promotion	\$ ....
Selling	\$ ....
Other	\$ ....
Total operating costs =	\$ ....

Now, consider how efficient your planned operation is. What things could you look at to increase your profitability? What costs might be reduced? By thinking through these things you will develop an insight into efficient nursery management.

9 Marketing

Marketing can make or break a nursery. There are many different ways of marketing nursery products. Some of the common systems are outlined below:

Retailing

Shops   These are garden centres or nurseries which concentrate on selling plants, or sections within other shops such as supermarkets, hardware stores or even florists.

Mail order   Usually promoted through catalogues and magazine advertisements.

Specialist nurseries   These concentrate on growing one particular type of plant which is sold direct to the public from the nursery. This type of nursery may wholesale plants also.

Shows   Trade shows, home shows, agricultural field days and other such events can be used as an outlet for selling plants.

Markets   Markets come in all types and sizes (e.g. craft markets, fruit and vegetable markets). Some nurseries find regular attendance at a market can make a significant contribution towards sales. Markets may also be used on an irregular basis to clear excess stock.

Wholesaling

Truck sales   A vehicle loaded with plants calls on retailers and usually sells direct from the truck. Some wholesalers use a smaller vehicle with samples of stock which are shown and orders are taken from.

Market   Trade markets conducted by industry associations or private markets which sell to retailers, landscapers and other industry people at wholesale prices. The organisers of these markets usually charge participating nurseries a fee or commission, or both.

Agents   These may sell using one or several different methods (e.g. truck sales, markets) and take a commission from the wholesale grower. This method can take away the worry of marketing, but it may also affect overall profit depending on how good or bad the agent is.

Marketing involves:
1. Publicising the products available (range, quality, diversity);
2. Packaging and presenting the goods or services;
3. Making contact with the person you are selling to;
4. Communication — ensuring your customers understand the goods or services;
5. Convincing — presenting the product in a way which favours you achieving the result you are aiming for;
6. Follow up — ensuring the buyer is satisfied with what they get (in the long term).

Products

The range and diversity of products available is an important issue for retailers. Wholesalers may require a certain diversity but certainly do not need it to the same extent as retailers. Retail customers expect to obtain an extensive range of plant and non-plant products from one outlet and prefer not to have to shop in a number of outlets. They will often choose a retail outlet that can cater to as many of their needs as possible. If you have competition nearby that can fulfil the customers' every need, you will either have to provide a similar range or specialise in something they do not cater for.

Examples of products and services that can be offered to customers include:

Plants
The majority of nursery sales are usually plants, seed or flowers. These can include natives, trees, shrubs, ground covers, climbers, perennials, herbs, bulbs, indoor plants, cacti, bonsai, topiary, potted colour, hanging baskets, terrariums, vegetable seedlings, berry plants, fruit trees, instant turf (sod), cut flowers, lawn seed, flower seed, vegetable seed, tree and shrub seed.

Allied products
These are products purchased to help grow plants better or to be used in landscaping. They provide add-on sales when customers buy plants and can include fertilisers, stakes, pots, mulch, soil additives, tree guards, chemical sprays, tools and equipment, horticultural fabrics, soils and potting media, hydroponic equipment, irrigation/watering equipment, garden buildings, fencing, rock and stone, masonry, concrete, timber, garden furniture, statues, ponds and pumps.

Services
Nursery staff may have the expertise to offer some special services either free or at a charge. Alternatively, they may develop a relationship with local 'experts' to provide such services. These services can include landscape design, delivering plants, identifying pest and disease problems, tree surgery, lawn repair, garden renovation, chemical spraying, routine garden maintenance, landscape construction, installing irrigation systems, erecting garden

Trade shows can be an excellent way to promote the nursery. (Lindsay Farr's Bonsai Farm display at Garden Week in Melbourne)

buildings, transplanting, pruning, recycling (refunds for used pots, chipping prunings, etc), entertainment (e.g. a guitar player or clown), a garden advice booth, and garden lectures or courses.

Other

There are a range of other things which may be included in nurseries to generate extra turnover. They need to be relevant to the type of nursery, and the type and number of customers attracted. They can include self-service drink or snack food machines, books, magazines, art and craft, cards, souvenirs, tea rooms, aquarium supplies, pet shop, hardware supplies, and pool and spa supplies.

Promotions

If a promotional campaign is to be successful, the following points must be achieved:

1. The different messages being presented should all relate to and support one common idea. If the common idea is that the nursery offers excellent service, for example, then every promotional exercise in a campaign should support this by saying the nursery has exceptional service 'because. . .' One advertisement might say the staff are very skilled. This could be followed by a press release saying the nursery will give a free plant to any customer who has to wait more than two minutes to be served. Both of these ideas share the same concept of service.

2. Different promotions must be identified quickly as being for the same nursery. This can be done by using the same colours on all literature, the same prominent logo or even the same type style in printing. Some nurseries achieve this by using the same voice or face on all advertisements.

Reaching customers

Every type of business is different, however, the following are some of the main ways of making contact with clients or customers:

- Local newspaper advertising
- Daily newspaper advertising
- Magazine advertising

- Letterbox drops
- Direct mail promotions
- Telephone directory
- Shopping centre displays
- Exhibitions/trade shows, etc.
- Radio/TV advertising
- Press releases
- Writing for newspapers, magazines, etc.
- Tender pages of magazines and newspapers
- Word of mouth — through friends, clubs, professional bodies, etc.
- Visiting — using a direct approach, i.e. sales reps calling on customers, or door knocking potential customers
- Telephone sales
- Establishing agents, e.g. local nurseries.

Promotions

The promotional edge is a combination of practical rules, 'flair', plus:
- the setting of sales-making objectives;
- effective presentation and display;
- control and measurement of sales and profits.

An important point. . .
Promotions can only work effectively if the basic merchandising job has been done properly. They are not a substitute for product range, siting and space allocation arrangements, and attractive displays.

Promotions can be used to achieve the following objectives:

1. Attract new customers to your nursery—to achieve this you need to clearly advertise or announce the promotion in your advertising.
2. Encourage customers to buy more when they visit your garden centre—to achieve this, mount feature displays on related products, e.g. if promoting rose food, feature an attractive display of roses.
3. Encourage customers to visit you for all their needs regularly—to achieve this, you need a planned and sustained program of promotions so that you always offer some inducement to your customers.

Timing of promotions
The horticulture industry operates on a very seasonal basis, so it is important to plan promotional activity for key products during the period of the year that generates the biggest demand. This is where suppliers can be helpful —

because they are the most familiar with their own product range, they are aware of the key selling months. Ask all major suppliers to submit a suggested promotional plan around which your own program can be organised.

Market Research

Know your market before you start! Successful marketing depends upon knowing the people/groups you are marketing to. You need to know:
• what they want;
• how they are likely to react to your product;
• what they will spend money on.

When the market place is understood, you can then follow the steps below to achieve successful marketing:
1. Set realistic marketing goals
2. Provide structures for reaching those goals
3. Assess the results of marketing efforts and modify your approaches accordingly

Market research involves all those activities which help management reach marketing decisions. It attempts to make unknown things known; and in most instances, largely succeeds.

Steps involved in market research
1. Define the problem to assess what information is required, e.g. ask yourself how you can increase sales by 10%.
2. Conduct an investigation. Examine past records which relate to the problem. Speak with people in the know, who might help with this problem. Try to find any relevant information which has been published (e.g. in trade magazines, Bureau of Statistics publications, etc).
3. If more information is required, you may decide to survey the customers (or potential customers). Note: this involves significantly more cost.
4. If the problem is still beyond you, you may employ a professional market research firm to handle it.

Types of market research
1. **Market research**   Determining needs and wants of prospective customers, assessing the potential of specific market areas, studying the competition, etc.
2. **Product research**   Looking into new product development, testing prices to determine if they are too high or low, etc. (e.g. you could keep an eye out for new Plant Variety Rights releases and their availability).
3. **Promotions research**   Checking effectiveness of displays or advertising, comparing cost-effectiveness of different publications by looking at advertising costs, types and numbers of readers, etc.
4. **Sales research**   Evaluating sales techniques of staff, looking at cost of selling, analysis of sales territory/distribution, etc. Cross reference sales to advertising if possible — the use of brochures may help in this respect.
5. **Company research**   Determining industry trends, determining the company's 'image' in the market place, studying employee morale or location of facilities. How do locals see your nursery for professionalism and service?

Ways of gathering data

There are two categories of information which might be researched:
1. Primary information — this is information not readily available and requires a real effort to discover.
2. Secondary information — this involves data which is readily available, but might require some investigation to bring the facts together.

Primary information
There are two main ways of gathering this data:
1. Asking people — this is known as the survey method.
2. Watching people — this is the observation method.
Another method, used less often, is the experimental method.

Survey method
• It is relatively inexpensive and adaptable to a wide variety of situations.
• Questions are asked through personal interviews, mail questionnaires, telephone interviews etc.
• Mail and telephone surveys are less expensive.
• Telephone surveys produce the quickest results but must be brief.
• Personal interviews are the most accurate.
• In a new nursery questions can help guide you to success.

Observation method

- Watch how people react to particular plants in flower, ornamental displays, etc.
- Cameras or tape recorders can be used to record reactions.
- Observations can be made of customers at point of sale.
- The main disadvantage of this method is that the observations may not be accurate.

Experimental method

Involves setting up a deliberate experiment (e.g. put one type of plants in one part of the nursery at one price, and similar plants in another part of the nursery at a different price and watch for the optimum balance to achieve good turnover and profit).

Secondary information

Always keep in mind:
- reliability of your source
- possibility of bias
- information they may be dated
- how applicable information is to a specific problem (it may have originally been gathered for some other reason)

Sources might include:
- Company records
- Government statistics
- Trade associations, institutes, etc.
- Research organisations (semi government)
- Trade/industry publications — there are many periodicals related to the nursery industry in Australia and overseas (see Appendix).

What do you need to research?

In any business, success is determined by a combination of many factors, and different factors are relevant in different situations. However, the following areas are commonly researched:

- Company policies — are company policies progressive or backward?
- Staff — are they helpful, courteous and efficient?
- After sales service — is it good or poor?
- Advertising/promotions — could these be improved?
- Cost of plants and other goods — are they expensive or inexpensive compared to other nurseries?

- Despatch of plants — is this carried out efficiently?
- Quality of plants on arrival.

Advertising budgets

The four main ways of determining an advertising budget are:

1. Affordable method Advertising is only carried out when the business can afford it. The major drawback with this approach is that it can lead to fluctuating advertising budgets, making long range planning very difficult.

2. Percentage of sales method This is based on a percentage of current or anticipated sales (either based on a percentage of each item sold or percentage of total dollars received). It is generally a better approach than the 'affordable method' because it bears a closer relationship to the movement of sales in the industry; it encourages management to think in terms of relationships between profit, advertising costs and sales price; and it encourages stability between competitors.

The major disadvantages are it discourages experimentation, and restricts long range planning because it is dependant on yearly fluctuations.

3. Competitive parity method The budget is set to match the competitors' activities. It has been claimed that the advantage of this approach is that it is based upon the collective wisdom of a particular sector of industry. However, there are no real reasons to believe that the opposition is more proficient than you!

4. Objective and task method This involves defining an objective to be achieved by advertising, then setting up an advertising program to meet that objective.

This might be done via the following steps:
- Establish a market share goal;
- Determine the percentage of the market share which needs to be reached;
- Determine the percentage of potential customers who need to be convinced to do business with your nursery;
- Determine the number of advertising exposures needed to get to attract one per cent of the population, i.e. how many copies of the advertisement, or how many times it is run on TV or radio);
- Determine the number of gross rating points

which would need to be obtained (a gross rating point is one exposure to one per cent of the potential buying population);
• Determine the advertising budget needed to achieve the purchase of one gross rating point.

Publicity Marketing

Publicity involves obtaining exposure for a product or service through the media, without directly paying for it. It may include:
• Press releases which lead to radio interviews or articles in newspapers.
• Conducting events or activities which attract media interest (such as product launches).

Publicity is based on the following principles:
1. Credibility
News or feature articles always appear more credible than an advertisement. If an article is written about a new product being introduced, this is a more credible way for someone to learn about that product than through an advertisement.
2. Catching people off guard
People who might avoid advertisements or other sales approaches will often read an article or listen to a news item about a product or service.
3. Dramatising products or services
Special, extraordinary events can be attached to product launches as a way of dramatising the product. For example, someone might be provided with the product to use on a round the world trip — this dramatises how the product could be used.

Press Releases

The following steps will help to promote your nursery's products or services through publication of press releases:

1. Understand the editor of the publication you are sending it to. Editors are most likely to print a press release in the following situations:
• When there is a gap in the publication which must be filled quickly, and your press release is the nearest thing at hand.
• When the press release fills a gap in the publication because it is the type of information the editor finds difficult to obtain.

• When the press release is about something in which the editor has a particular interest.
2. Be aware that the editor might drastically change or reduce your press release if he or she is not totally happy with what you send in. Changes are usually better made by you, so try to get it right before sending it.
3. It must capture the interest of readers to work. To do this you must understand the readers:
• Some publications have a readership which reads every article thoroughly.
• Others have readers which tend to look at the pictures and only read the headings of articles unless the article draws their attention.
4. The heading is critical — it must grab the reader's attention.
5. The first sentence must grab the reader's attention and clearly relate to the article. After reading the first sentence the reader will decide whether to read on or stop.
6. The article should be written in such a way that it will still make sense if some sections are taken out. An editor may only have space for something smaller.
7. Clarity is very important. All types of people should be able to understand your message. Avoid big or difficult words. Keep it simple.
8. Conciseness is extremely important. Always use the minimum number of words. Look over what you have written and rewrite it to use less words wherever possible.
9. A press release can be as little 60 to 100 words, or as much as 1000 or more words. Generally smaller press releases are more likely to be printed.
10. Present press releases as a double spaced, typed document, on white paper with the words 'Press Release' written at the top.
11. Include a photograph (a black and white print or colour slide) if possible. This is often very worthwhile, but by no means necessary.
12. Don't make it sound like an advertisement. Publishers will not print press releases that sound too much like free ads. Your company's name, contact person, address and phone number should be included for further information but your promotion must be subtle.
13. Post press releases to newspapers 1-2 weeks before publication, and to magazines 3-4 months before publication. A faxed press release can be sent

to radio and TV stations a few days before you hope to have them broadcast your article.

Packaging

Packaging is the way a product is presented for sale. In this regard a retail nursery will be quite different to a wholesale nursery. In a retail nursery the customer sees everything (or almost everything), so every plant should be in perfect condition, and floors, shelves and display units should be clean and neat. In a wholesale nursery the customer might not see much of the nursery, so even though cleanliness is important, the nursery don't always have to look so perfect.

Presentation of retail nurseries

Fixtures and fittings
They have a considerable impact on the character or image which your nursery presents. You may decide to choose and set these up yourself, or you can use the services of specialised shopfitting companies or tradesmen trained in shopfitting. If you do it yourself, remember that just because you made your home look good doesn't mean you can do the same in a shop. Shops are very different!

Layout
Retail shops are usually divided into three areas:
1. Major product areas (also called 'point of sales areas' — see page 118)
The most popular products are placed in prominent positions to encourage further sales. These areas include window displays, and displays which can obviously be seen from the front door and the counter (i.e. places which will be seen clearly by everyone who comes into the shop).
2. Departments
Products which relate to each other are best grouped together (e.g. in a retail nursery, seedlings are put into one area, and indoor plants are put into a different area). It is generally preferable for adjacent departments to relate to each other (e.g. fruit trees are better located next to a stand selling fertilisers and chemicals rather than ornamental pots).

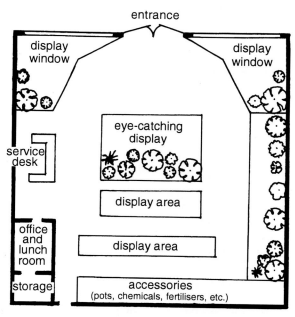

Layout of a small retail plant shop

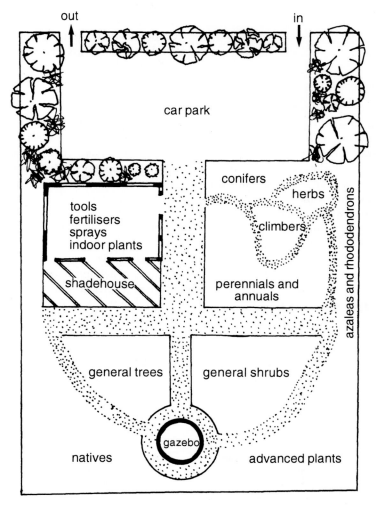

Layout of a retail nursery

3. Service area

This is the main counter from which people are served. This area usually includes a cash register, credit card facilities, brochures and wrapping facilities. It should be located in a position from which all parts of the shop are visible, and for both service and security reasons it is generally best located near to entry/exit points.

What Sells Best

1. Products at point of sale locations. Examples of point of sale positions are:
- The main counter beside the till
- The ends of rows
- Islands in open parts of a showroom floor
- Points close to the entry and exit
- Window displays

2. Products placed at eye level. These tend to sell better than those placed below or above eye level.

3. Products displayed en masse. Twenty of the same plant in a group will create an immediate impact, while one plant mixed amongst other varieties may go unnoticed.

4. Products with large signs which highlight their selling point, e.g. if you think a discounted price will sell the product, then you need a large sign with the product saying 'Discount'.

5. Colourful displays

6. Well lit areas. When placing lights, you should consider the following points:
- Some areas may be shadowed
- Artificial lights may distort colours
- Point of sale locations should be highlighted with extra lighting
- Avoid creating glare from unshaded light globes
- Light fixtures must fit the decor

Spacing

Customers shy away from cluttered, confined spaces. If products are displayed with plenty of space both between the products and in the surrounding area, then that part of the shop is more likely to be visited.

Aisles should be wide enough for people to pass in, although they should not be too long. People should be able to get out of one aisle to go to the next without having to walk very long distances.

Quantity displayed

A well stocked nursery will appear successful and inspire confidence in the customer. However, it is best to avoid cluttering items and to leave a space between different lines so customers can easily find and remove the product without a creating a mass landslide!

Take notice where people stop and look at things

Tiered shelves are an attractive way to display plants in the retail nursery.

in your nursery, and try to determine why this is so. Also notice 'dead' areas, and try to determine what can be done to attract people into those parts of the nursery.

Signs

Many people like to make their own decisions with minimal help from salespeople. Thus signposting is one of the most important communicating tools with customers in a nursery. They are cheaper than employees because they don't get sick, they don't ask for pay increases, and they work all the time.

A professional signwriter should be employed for at least one or two major signs. If expense is a factor other signs may be obtained the following ways:

1. Free signs — product suppliers will often provide posters, display signs, etc. free of charge.

2. Ready-made signs — shopfitting or stationery suppliers can supply some ready-made signs (e.g. OPENING SALE, DISCOUNTS, PAY HERE, DO NOT TOUCH, etc).

3. Stencils — stationery wholesalers or companies listed under 'Signs' in the phone book can often supply stencils or stick-on lettering of varying sizes to make your own signs. Signs made this way are particularly effective if laminated (see the phone book for laminating companies). Laminating is a process where card or paper is permanently sealed between two layers of plastic.

4. Standard banners — these can be supplied at reasonable prices by banner makers.

It is important to write the signs from a customer's point of view and make sure all information is given to enable them to make a buying decision. You should also remember that every sign reflects your nursery's image and your knowledge.

The advantages of signs are that they provide an excellent training program for new employees, as well as giving information to customers. The disadvantages are they require time for development and maintenance and can be an expensive outlay. (NB. 80% of customers wait on themselves and 80% of customers' plant questions can be answered with the use of signs. Every plant should have certain information, i.e. why the customer should buy it, what it will do for them, how to plant and care for it, and how much it will cost them.)

Hints for writing signs and plant labels

- Always tell the truth
- Make sure it is readable
- Use layperson's terms
- Assume the customer has no knowledge of the plant
- Present information the customer wants to know
- Explain words and activities that suggest special knowledge
- Be consistent in size and placement of signs

Packaging in Wholesale Nurseries

Above all, plants need to be packaged in such a way that they are not damaged in transit. Other aspects such as staking, the type of container and labelling are of secondary importance. However, these things can make a difference to sales, particularly when plants are being sold to retailers for resale. The retailer will always appreciate packaging which is easier to handle and which can be displayed for sale with the minimum of fuss.

Wrapping: Individual plants may be wrapped in cellophane sleeves to protect foliage and to improve the plant's appearance. This is often done for indoor plants and 'potted colour'.

Labelling: Tubestock is often sold with only one or two labels to a tray, and this may be appropriate where plants are to be repotted or planted in nursery rows for growing on. When plants are sold to retailers each individual plant should be labelled.

Everything else being equal, retailers will tend to buy plants with better quality labels. Some wholesalers even supply point of sale material to retailers, such as posters, information sheets or display tags with a photograph and basic cultural information. This type of service makes life easier for the retailer, and generally improves sales for both the wholesale grower and the retailer.

Containers: It is better to standardise containers for particular lines, in terms of colour and size. Some nurseries will grow one type of plant in one size container and others in a different size. Perennials and herbs are often grown in smaller containers or even square containers, while trees and shrubs in the same nursery might be grown in larger containers. Some nurseries colour code their plants; for example, natives are grown in one coloured container, trees in another colour, and shrubs in yet another.

The choice of container is, of course, influenced by what is best for plant growth, but these marketing considerations are also very important.

Stakes and trellises: Climbers require a stake or small trellis with each plant to prevent the stems intermingling with neighbouring plants. Other plants may require stakes to support weak stems or to help train growth. The type of stake or trellis used can add significantly to the cost of production, but depending on the type chosen it can also greatly improve the marketability of the plant.

Boxes and trays: These are used to move plants about. They are made from wood, plastic, metal or cardboard (usually waxed for waterproofing). The cost can be considerable and some wholesalers choose to recycle trays and boxes, asking customers to return them (perhaps using a deposit/refund system). When plants are sent through freight services recycling can be difficult to implement.

Some boxes are not particularly attractive, having been designed to simply move plants easily and safely. Other boxes are designed to display plants in a retail situation. This type of box can help boost sales significantly, but it will also add to production costs and inevitably mean a higher retail price.

Transport

Nurseries need to move plants from the seller to the customer. Transport can be either handled by the nursery, or subcontracted to carriers (e.g. trucking companies, rail, or even the mail in some cases). Whatever method is used attention must be given to moving plants fast, at a competitive price, and without causing any damage.

Retail nurseries which visit wholesalers or markets to buy plants will need an appropriate vehicle or trailer to bring plants home, and even those who don't will probably need transport to deliver plants to customers who don't have their own transport.

Wholesale nurseries will require a vehicle or vehicles to deliver plants to retail customers, or even when using rail services, to deliver to the railway station.

Some plants, such as bulbs, perennials, and deciduous trees and shrubs, go through a dormant period when they are far less susceptible to being damaged in transit. The production and marketing of these plants is usually timed to coincide with the dormant period. They are usually cheaper to ship and more economically viable to package because they can be shipped without soil, and numbers of plants can be packaged together.

Plants which are transported with soil around their roots must be packed in a way which will ensure the plant remains in good condition. Be careful that plants do not move in transit, tipping soil from containers or damaging foliage. Plants which are in transit for several days in hot weather may dry out and suffer serious stress. Even if a customer has prepaid, return business will be unlikely if plants are damaged in transit.

Quarantine regulations between states and countries restrict the movement of both soil and plant material. If you are shipping interstate or internationally, check the regulations first. In some cases it is necessary to obtain permits.

Plants in tissue culture are generally an easier method of transporting plants, especially if importing into Australia.

Paperwork is important when shipping. Accurate records must be kept of what is shipped out and what is received at the other end by the buyer.

Sales

Wholesaling plants

Wholesalers can sell to customers in the following ways:
* Taking orders to grow (contract growers)
* Calling on retailers (sales reps)
* At trade days/wholesale markets
* Through agents
* Franchising (buying/leasing the right to sell a company's plants or services in a particular area)
* Direct sales to retailers, landscapers and councils

Retailing plants

A summary of the alternatives:
Mail Order   A low cost alternative which involves selling plants and associated services/goods through the mail. This method bypasses some of the

Selling plants at a small community weekend market. Few nursery growers make a fortune this way, but many begin like this.

problems and expenses associated with retail outlets (e.g. you don't need to buy or lease a sales outlet in an area which will attract customers). Advertising and promotional work needs to be done to gain customers who send away for your goods.

Markets May be a one-off stand or a contract stand depending on the market. Markets are a good way of selling poor quality or end-of-line stock. They are also a convenient sales outlet for backyard growers. Competitive prices are expected by customers. Not all markets are open during the week, although most are open on weekends.

Shops The common retail alternative. The shop may be a large garden centre/nursery or a small shop in a shopping centre. Many costs are involved in running a shop but it is accessible to the public.

Party plans A form of selling products to a group of people. Organisation is done through a host who provides the venue as well as drinks and nibbles for the guests. If a certain amount of produce is sold, then the host receives a 'gift', e.g. a plant of his or her choice.

Hawking Selling from a vehicle or trailer on the roadside. Few costs are involved, although sales are dependant on passing traffic. Most local councils require a hawking licence to be obtained for a specific area.

The Salesperson

Staff are the greatest asset of any business. Even if you have the best retail site, the best store layout, the best range of products and the most competitive range of products, your business won't work if you have poorly presented, ignorant and uncaring sales staff.

Every salesperson should know:
• Details of the product or service — its attributes, drawbacks, and competing products.
• Where and how to find the product/brochures/catalogues/order forms or anything else relating to the sale.
• The prices to charge and terms of sale.
• Procedure for making a sale (including using a cash register, filling out the order book, writing receipts, etc).
• Company policies on returns and damaged goods.
• How to package or deliver goods or services.
• How to keep records in order.
• How to maintain order in the sales area.

A good salesperson should possess the following characteristics:
• A good appearance
• A pleasant personality
• Courtesy and tact
• Ability to enjoy selling
• A basic understanding of human nature (practical not theoretical, i.e the ability to read people's body language)

Key rules every salesperson should follow
• Research your customer and product first. (You need to know both the customer and the product before you attempt to sell.)
• Find out your customer's full shopping list before you start dealing. Gently introduce them to products that will complement the ones they want, e.g. if they buy an orchid plant, they will require a special orchid mix. Remember that most customers are open to suggestions and want their plants to grow well so you should help them achieve these goals.
• Highlight the benefits of a product rather than the features. (Tell the customer what it can do for them personally — don't tell them what is great and unique about the product if it is not relevant to them in particular.)
• If there are objections, play it cool and try to determine very specifically what they are. Once you narrow down the objection, put it into perspective by showing something about the product which compensates that objection (e.g. 'Yes it is expensive but it will grow better in your soil'). Don't make it seem as if you have won a point.
• Always keep control of the conversation — don't let yourself get into a defensive position. This is done by asking questions when the customer starts to take the offensive.
• Do not talk while giving a demonstration. Show them, then stop and talk.
• Handle products with respect.
• Get the customer to try out the product.
• If you need to, use the phone or calculator to buy thinking time.
• Try to close the sale—ask for an order at the appropriate time, when the customer seems to be in a state of mind where he or she is likely to buy.
• Fulfilling the customer's needs is more important than improving your own knowledge or sales technique.

• Remember that the customer is always right — without their patronage you are not going to remain in business.

Plant knowledge is one of the most important requirements of sales staff in nurseries. This can be a disadvantage for new staff with little plant knowledge. If you or your staff have this problem, remember it is better to keep the customer waiting for a short period while the information is being researched rather than giving the customer incorrect information. Signs around the nursery will also help here.

Aftersales service

Selling is one skill, but inspiring a customer to come back and buy again is something else. A new customer is great but a regular customer is gold and needs to be looked after. This is where aftersales service comes in.

Aftersales service in retail nurseries
• Develop relationships with customers by keeping them advised of new products, specials and reduced pricelines; especially in areas they are interested in.
• Provide opportunities for 'valued customers' to preview sale items, new products, etc.
• Give discounts for big sales and invite the buyer to discounted workshops and lectures.
• Give away 'freebies' and provide free delivery services to help increase customer goodwill.
• Operate a a free garden advice service to current and former customers. This can be used for retail and wholesale nurseries.
• Give a six month to one year guarantee on all your plant produce and six months of free advice. The small cost will pay off in the long term through customer satisfaction and positive word-of-mouth advertising. Lace this with a complimentary tea or coffee if they are visiting the nursery.

Aftersales service in wholesale nurseries
• Wholesale nurseries should have a plant list which is sent out to customers.
• Regular customers should be phoned to determine their stock supply. This might happen every one to two months.
• Keep a filing system where plant varieties, quantities bought, and when they were bought can be easily accessed.

• Call valued customers and see if they need similar stock and quantities as bought last month/year. Introduce them to new products that are ready at this time.
• Do some homework with regard to plant popularity and keep up with consumer trends, so new plants grown will be good sellers. The key is to keep one step in front of your customers.

Questionnaires are an excellent way of finding out problem areas within a company. Use a suggestion box for written questionnaires or phone customers to check satisfaction levels with plants, quality and service. Use the information constructively. Discuss improvements with dissatisfied customers and encourage continued custom by rectifying any problems. Give personal service, refunds, exchange products, etc.

Newsletters are an excellent way to keep customers informed about what is happening in the nursery. It could cover new staff, staff profiles, new products, company policies, company changes/expansions, etc. Use it as an informative handout rather than for target marketing. Newsletters help make customers feel part of the 'family'.

Customer satisfaction should be the main aim in business. If good service is given before and after the sale then your costs will decrease as word of mouth advertising spreads. Happy customers come back. Advertising and promotions are always needed to retain present customers and gain new ones.

Legal Implications of Marketing

The nursery manager must consider the legal implications of selling plants. It is not a simple case of growing a plant and selling it. The customer has legal rights, and so do you as the grower or retailer.

Laws are generally thought of as rules which should not be broken. This is so with criminal law, however business law is different. Business laws are set guidelines by which people are able to enter binding agreements which, in return for some 'advantage', they voluntarily enter into a stated 'obligation'. This is 'contract law'.

All contracts begin with a promise. (All promises are not contracts though.) A contract does not exist until the parties involved reach agreement on what is being given and what is to be accepted by each of those parties concerned.

If the seller has breached the conditions of a contract, the buyer is normally entitled to rescind the contract, return the goods and receive a full refund.

Warranty and Condition

Under law, a warranty is a minor or non essential term in a contract. A condition is a major or essential term.

Most nurseries will guarantee their stock is true to name and in healthy condition at the time of sale. Some retail nurseries will offer a warranty on their plants for 6-12 months, while others will not be held responsible for the plant's condition after it is transplanted.

Consumer laws

Awareness of consumer laws is important in both wholesale and retail nurseries. The end result is that you are selling a product to a consumer, whether the consumer is a retail nursery, a landscaper, or a retail customer.

There are a number of Acts of Parliament which provide consumer protection. Generally these laws guarantee the consumer four basic rights as follows:
1. Safety — that the goods are safe to use.
2. Knowledge — the buyer has the right to have sufficient knowledge about the goods or services purchased to ensure consumer protection against physical harm, to prevent the consumer damaging or misusing the goods purchased, and to prevent the consumer from buying things which he or she does not need.

Most nurseries provide extensive information on individual plants so customers know the conditions needed to grow that plant. The customer can then ask for more information or make intelligent decisions on the information provided regarding other secondary products (e.g. fertiliser, growing media).
3. Choice — the buyer must have the right to choose which product he or she wishes to purchase.
4. Complaints — the buyer has the right to express any complaints. It is worthwhile either conducting a survey or having a 'complaints' box. Wholesale

nurseries sometimes send out brief survey sheets with their catalogue to regular customers.

Normally if there is a problem with a product, it must be dealt with between the parties who are involved in the contract (e.g. if a friend has problems with a chainsaw you purchased and cut himself due to improper manufacturing, the friend cannot sue for damages — he was not part of the initial contract).

The purchaser will normally sue the seller. In turn of course, the seller may then sue the manufacturer.

Even though this is the normal case, courts have sometimes allowed the manufacturer to be sued by the consumer when a collateral contract is considered. This is a situation where a retailer has purchased from a manufacturer where the purchase was made based upon statements made by the manufacturer which were not complied with.

In order for a manufacturer to be shown liable, it must be shown that:
1. He/she owed the affected person (who is complaining) a duty to be careful.
2. He/she breached his/her duty to by failing to take care in manufacture.
3. The lack of care by the manufacturer caused damages to the buyer.

Developing a Marketing Program

The following is an example of just one approach a nursery might take to implement a marketing program.

Marketing plan for GreenPlant Wholesale Nursery

1.0 General

The project is based primarily on the development of a wholesale nursery, which will market the plants it produces. Secondary (after establishing initial markets for the nursery) marketing activities might involve selling additional products or services which develop as the project proceeds (e.g. tourism developments and landscaping services).

2.0 Market Identification and Definition

Although the various activities of the project will share some common markets, for the sake of simplicity this plan will be organised on the basis of each activity. The major markets covered here include sectors of the regional wholesale and retail plant markets.

2.1 Wholesale Nursery

With the need to first develop production skills among the nursery staff, access to some temporary markets will be necessary. That is, production will necessarily commence with easier, general nursery varieties.

At least 15–20% of manpower should be devoted to marketing from the commencement of the project. It is likely that since requirements for office staff will be relatively minor in the early stages of production, staff designated for these positions could be involved in marketing activities.

Marketing will mainly involve the following:
1. Selling plants

Plants may be sold any of the following ways:
• Seeking advance orders for contract growing.(e.g. through chain stores, growing-on nurseries and government departments).
• Selling from stands at trade shows, agricultural shows, markets, etc.
• Selling to people who visit the nursery site.
• Selling through agents.
• Receiving phone calls from, and dealing with people who have heard of the nursery through promotional activities.
• Repeat trade from previous customers.
• Making direct contact with targeted customers (e.g. contact herb nurseries to sell herbs or native nurseries to sell natives).
• Putting plants into other outlets on a sale or return basis.
• By doing the rounds of nurseries for direct sales.
• Mail order sales.

2. Promoting the nursery
• Through press releases.
• Through paid advertisements.
• Through stands at shows.
• By phone or direct mail to potential customers.
• Through catalogues/stock lists.
• Through involvement in trade organisations or marketing service groups.

• Taking and processing orders. This involves routine jobs including:
a. Taking an order over the phone, by fax, in person or through the mail;
b. Getting the plants together for a delivery;
c. Labelling the plants;
d. Packaging;
e. Making deliveries.

2.2 Tourist-related Activities

Once the garden and nursery sales are established, attention can then be turned towards marketing to the tourist industry. At this point in time, the project will have the potential to offer the following to tourists:
• Sales of plants produced in the nursery
• Tours of the nursery and garden
• Display gardens, perhaps containing a maze and picnic facilities.

Other services for tourists can then be added to these. A service/shop area should be located adjacent to the office. This way it is possible for the same person who looks after the office to also attend to visitors.

Development of this market will require the use of regional publications and special interest groups. Information, and perhaps also some product sales, should also be available in regional tourist information centres, motels and other places visited by tourists in the area. Enquiries with the local Chamber of Commerce should assist in locating such places and determining their best utilisation.

3.0 Direct Nursery Sales from the Site

This can be developed early (but no earlier than six months from commencing propagation). Direct plant sales can commence well before the tourist market is developed.

Some of the initial stock can be potted into larger pots to sell direct to the public, for example 100–125 mm round pots. These size pots are readily marketable to tourists. Permits from council may be needed for direct sales.

Some signs and leaflets will also be needed (e.g. a sandwich board placed by the main road to direct traffic to the nursery). The nursery could also be promoted through the local paper.

The direct sales area should initially be small and well maintained, with public access to other areas restricted.

4.0 Equipment for Marketing

To conduct efficient marketing the business will need the following:

• A fax — this is important for rapid communications with customers and suppliers. Many nurseries send their orders by this method. This should be purchased as soon as possible when revenue from plant sales is sufficient.

• Telephone

• A word processor — for production of up-to-date stock lists, correspondence and billing.

• Transport — something to transport plants in (e.g. a covered in tandem trailer with racks or large covered in truck)

• Signs

• Business cards

• Promotional leaflets and catalogues

• Printed labels

5.0 Marketing Timetable

Stage 1

During the first six months of nursery operations the following should be done:

• Advertise the business as a tubestock propagation nursery in trade magazines.

• Send out press releases every 6-8 weeks; initially as 'news items' telling how the project was started and how it is developing.

• Design, make up and print general promotional brochures.

• Compile stock lists of plants in production (on word processor).

• Direct mail promotional leaflets, stock lists and covering letters to growing-on nurseries, in advance of plants being ready for sale.

• Make direct contact by phone, and by visiting potential customers (e.g. government departments and growing-on nurseries).

• Design a series of signs for use on site, at markets, and in shows.

• Join one or more trade organisations.

Stage 2

After nursery stock is beginning to increase and excess produce is becoming available for sale through the community garden:

• Continue with the marketing activities started in stage 1.

• Obtain council permission and place signs on the main roads and at the front of the property to direct people onto the property for direct sales.

• Commence advertising direct to the public sales through general magazines.

• Commence selling at markets and promoting/selling through trade shows and exhibitions.

• Experiment with other avenues of marketing and develop marketing in those areas which are most successful.

Stage 3

Once nursery markets begin to establish, and sufficient profitability and cash flow are achieved, attention can then be turned to developing and marketing the tourist side of the business.

• Advertising would be broadened and expanded to target the tourist industry.

• Two separate promotional campaigns should be run, one targeting the people who buy plants from the wholesale nursery; the other targeting the tourist industry and the general public. The results from each program should be monitored and adjustments made to each program accordingly, on an annual basis.

10 Developing a Nursery Stock List

One of the most important decisions for any nursery to make is what type of plants should be grown and/or bought from other nurseries to sell.

Considering the options

The first decision is whether to specialise or not. A nursery can specialise in terms of the plant varieties grown, or in terms of the size of plants grown. Some nurseries grow a wide variety of plants but only in the one size container, or perhaps only in the open ground (where they are dug up and balled or potted before selling). Other nurseries might concentrate on one particular group of plants (e.g. herbs or natives), but they might grow and sell those plants in a variety of sizes and containers. Some growers choose to be even more specific, selling only one genus of plants (e.g. fuchsias, geraniums, carnations).

There is a very real danger in choosing what to grow on a whim or a fancy. It is not a good business decision to specialise in something just because that is what you like! Just because you like that particular type of plant doesn't mean that many others will, or if there are several people who have the same attitude and make the same decision in the same locality, then supply of that type of plant is likely to exceed demand.

Developing a plant list should be an ongoing task.

Plant varieties should be added to and removed from your list continually. The numbers grown or stocked should also be increased or reduced regularly. An annual assessment (at the minimum) should be made of what has sold, what has not sold, and what has been requested or ordered.

Someone new to the industry may need to experiment to find their niche. Remember 'in fashion' plants that you read about in magazines and see everywhere are sometimes being grown or sold by every other new nurseryperson, so there might be a lot of competition.

It is also important to remember that many of the newer varieties being widely sold are protected by plant variety rights or patents, so it is illegal to sell them unless you have an agreement/licence with the owner of the rights.

Retail nurseries and garden centres

Retail nurseries may cater to either a local or regional market. Small nurseries generally cater to a local area. When the local area is new and there is a lot of building activity, these nurseries will tend to sell large numbers of fast-growing trees and shrubs. There will normally be a demand for all types of plants, so the nursery should stock a wide variety of plants. The exception to this is where the housing in the area is based on a particular theme, or local government planning controls restrict development with the object of maintaining indigenous plants.

In some countries or localities a certain style of

garden might be more popular, so plants needed for that type of garden will be in greater demand. In built-up areas with smaller properties or flats and units, smaller plants will probably be more in demand. Indoor plants, hanging baskets and container plants will probably be in greater demand in densely populated areas than in rural areas.

Once an area becomes established, the local nursery will find more sales in plants used to maintain or renovate established gardens. Smaller ornamental and flowering plants, groundcovers and annual seedlings can become a more important stock item. Anyone establishing or taking over a local retail nursery will find it useful to visit similar sized nurseries in similar localities to see what mix of plant varieties are being stocked.

Larger retail nurseries can cater to a regional market, attracting people from a wider field. If located in a prominent position (e.g. a main road) or promoted in an appropriate way, this type of nursery can draw all types of customers wanting nearly any type of plant. Specialist sections can be incorporated into the nursery and promoted to a specific market (e.g. an orchid section selling and displaying a wide range of orchids might be promoted widely amongst orchid enthusiasts to attract these people to the nursery).

Wholesale nurseries
Wholesale nurseries, and sometimes wholesale/retail nurseries, often specialise in a particular group of plants. The following are common types of specialisations:

Trees, shrubs and groundcovers; flower and vegetable seedlings; natives; ferns; conifers; herbs; indoor plants; fruit trees; natives; orchids; water plants; perennials and rockery plants; palms rainforest plants; budded and grafted plants.

Specialist Nurseries
Most regions or countries have small numbers of more highly specialised nurseries. These nurseries often service an entire country, or even an international market. The market is rarely big enough even in a large city to sustain this type of specialist nursery without marketing its plants more widely. This type of nursery often sells plants both retail and wholesale, or wholesale only. They might deal with only one particular genus (or mainly one genus). Typical nurseries of this type might specialise in one of the following plant groups:

Roses, bonsai, fuchsias, proteas, azaleas and rhododendrons, chrysanthemums, daisies, liliums, iris, cacti, pelargoniums, impatiens, African violets, camellias.

Some nurseries combine a number of different but compatible specialist types of plants, in that way buffering against any unforseen drop in demand for one of the types they grow. Examples of combinations are:
Azaleas, rhododendrons and camellias
Ferns and orchids
Herbs and perennials
Deciduous fruit and ornamental trees
Bulbs and perennials
Proteas and banksias

To remain competitive, nurseries should be prepared to evolve over time. This means changing what they specialise in as demands/trends change.

Criteria for selecting plants

When deciding what plants to grow or stock in a nursery, you should take into consideration the following criteria:

1. Ease of propagation
Is it very easy, of average ease, or difficult to propagate? Plants which are very easy to propagate may bring a lower wholesale price, and their supply in the marketplace might be greater. Difficult plants may be more costly to produce, and more risky to get a profit from unless you have better than average skills.

2. Availability of stock
Can it always be purchased in the form you want (e.g. seed, tube stock, advanced plants)? If the propagation material is to be imported you will need to consider quarantine restrictions.

3. Time needed to grow the plant
Some plants can be ready to sell within months, others take many years. Plants that can be produced and sold quickly will generate income quickly.

4. Suitability to your facilities
Do you have the right buildings, propagation equipment and other facilities to grow the particular plants under consideration? Do you have the money and the space to provide those facilities?

5. Suitability of climate
What plants are most suitable to grow in your

climate? It is always more efficient to work with the environment rather than trying to modify environments.

6. Distance from potential markets
Transport is costly, and can be risky.

7. Your staff's skills
Don't try to do what you or your staff are not skilled to do. Someone with more experience or specialised skills will probably do it better and cheaper.

Developing a stock list

There are many different ways of developing a nursery stock list. The following method is just one example.

1. Decide on the following big questions first.

• How will plants be sold?
Wholesale..... Retail.... Wholesale and Retail..... Mail Order.....

• How will plants be sold and in what size?
Cuttings/Seedlings..... Tubestock..... Small pots..... Standard or medium pots..... Advanced containers..... Bare-rooted..... Balled..... Other........................

• How many plants will be sold annually?
Number..... Gross value $.....

• Which types of plants will be sold and what percentage of nursery turnover will be devoted to each group?

% of total grown

Native plants	....
Indoor plants	....
Seedlings	....
Deciduous trees	....
Herbs	....
General trees and shrubs	....
Perennials	....
Cacti and succulents	....
Orchids	....
Rhododendrons/Azaleas/ Camellias	....
Ferns	....
Roses	....
Other	....

2. Visit at least two different nurseries which sell the types of plants you plan to sell. Start to compile a list of the plant varieties which are being sold by both of these nurseries. These are likely to be the more saleable varieties.

3. Look through gardening magazines, nursery catalogues and trade journals to determine which of the varieties on your list are mentioned most frequently, and whether any other varieties of plants seem to occur in the literature frequently.

4. Consider the marketability of your selected plants. Some plants are far more superior as 'turnover plants' than others. Use the criteria below if you wish to categorise each plant you consider.
a) Very highly marketable (VHM)
Traditionally and currently these plants have sold very well at most times of the year.
b) Highly marketable (HM)
Sell very well but only at certain times of the year.
c) Good standard line provided you do not grow too many (GSL)
d) Usually sells well provided the quality is good (USW)
We suggest you limit such varieties to not more than 2% of your total production.
e) Requires some effort to sell, but normally a reasonable line provided quality is good and quantity is not too high (RSE)
We suggest that you should limit this line to not more than 0.25% of your total production.
f) Often a poor seller (PS)
g) High risk variety (HR)
These plants may do very well or may do very poorly. They should be treated as a speculative crop.

Presentation

When considering the marketability of a plant, you should take into account all of the following aspects. Consider what is the normal and acceptable way to sell the variety in question. Sometimes you can do better selling it in a different way to what is 'normal', but the customers may be preconditioned to buying particular varieties in particular pot sizes, at a certain time of year and looking a certain way.

The following system or something similar can be used to indicate the way each plant on your plant list should be presented to the market.

Packaging

2 in.. two inch (= 50 mm) tube
4 in.. 4 inch (= 100 mm) plastic pot
5in.. 5 inch (= 125 mm) plastic pot
5-6 in.. 5 to 6 inch (= 125-150 mm) plastic pot
Pun.. punnets

Bare.. bare rooted
Bal.. balled
Bsk.. basket plant

Presentation

Fl.. sell when in flower only
Pic.. pictoral label is very important
Il.. inexpensive label, only correct naming is really important
St.. normally sold tied to a stake
Trel.. normally sold tied to a trellis

Marketing time

Sum/Win/Aut/Spr.. This indicates the months of the year when this plant is released in retail outlets.

5. Determine the relative quantities of different varieties which you should aim to stock or sell. Delete any plants from the list which you are uncertain about (in terms of either your ability to produce or obtain them, or your ability to sell them). The final list should now be viewed as a general guide for either obtaining stock for a retail nursery, or growing plants in a wholesale nursery. It will be varied and adapted to changing conditions in the marketplace as time goes by.

Stock List for Plant Type: Trees (example)

Plant Variety	Marketa-bility	Packag-ing	Presenta-tion	Marketing Time	Annual Stock Numbers
Acacia baileyana	VHM	2in	Il	Aut/Win	2,000
Betula alba	HM	Bare	Pic	Win	750
Cedrus atlantica glauca	GS	Bal	Pic	Win/ Spr	400

The next step

Once a basic stocklist has been established it is essential that the nursery keeps track of plants. A good nursery manager will know numbers of each type of plant bought or propagated, the numbers lost through death or being thrown out, and the numbers sold. Nurseries are increasingly able to use modern technology such as bar coding and computers to record this type of information.

Initially it will take a considerable effort to compile a stock list, but it should be done before investing any major amounts of money in either purchasing or growing plants. It can make a significant difference.

Appendixes

Further Information

Courses

The Australian Correspondence Schools conduct more than 150 different home study courses, including eleven courses designed for people who work, or would like to work, in nurseries. These range from courses for people who propagate plants at home as a small part-time business, to courses designed for managers or owners of large commercial operations. The three certificates offered are all government accredited, and as such well accepted by both industry and other educational institutions.

Courses offered include:

Short Courses: Propagation, Advanced Propagation, Tissue Culture, Nursery Growers Course, Nursery Hands Course, Soil Management (Nurseries), Garden Centre Management, Wholesale Nursery Management.

Accredited Certificates: Certificate in Horticulture (Propagation), Advanced Certificate in Applied Management (Retail Nursery), Advanced Certificate in Applied Management (Wholesale Nursery).

The Nursery Growers Course is an 80-hour introductory course for people starting a small, part-time business, growing and selling plants. This is a course for the inexperienced grower only.

Garden Centre Management and Wholesale Nursery Management are 120-hour courses, each providing a basic training for nurserypersons who might not have the time to pursue a full certificate.

The Certificate in Horticulture (Propagation) is similar to other horticulture certificates in its introductory (core) units, but devotes 50% of the course to quite different topics specifically related to propagation. Designed principally for plant propagators, this course deals with hundreds of different types of plants and the methods used to propagate them.

The Advanced Certificate in Applied Management (Retail Nursery) is devoted equally to developing management and horticultural skills for a supervisor or manager in a retail nursery or garden centre. The key areas of study are Communications, Management, Office Practices, Business Operations, Marketing, Plant Identification and Culture, Nursery Plant Stock, Nursery Production Systems and Equipment, Display & Display Techniques and Garden Product Knowledge (Hardware).

The Advanced Certificate in Applied Management (Wholesale Nursery) covers Communications, Management, Office Practices, Business Operations, Marketing, Plant Identification and Culture, Propagation, and Nursery Production Systems and Equipment.

Other certificate and non-certificate courses are offered in related disciplines including Herbs, Horticultural Technology, Landscaping, Small Business, Supervision and Marketing, Computer Studies, Irrigation, and Soil Management.

For further details contact:
Australian Correspondence Schools
PO Box 2092, Nerang East, Queensland, Australia,
4211 Phone/Fax: (075) 304 855
264 Swansea Rd, Lilydale, Victoria, Australia, 3140
Phone/Fax: (03) 736 1882

Further Reading

The following publications are highly recommended for further reading.

Other titles by the author of this book:
Mason J., *Starting A Nursery or Herb Farm*, Night Owl Publishers, Australia, 1983
Mason J., *Growing Ferns*, Kangaroo Press, Australia, 1990
Mason J., *The Native Plant Expert*, Australian Horticultural Correspondence School, Australia, 1989
Mason J., *Commercial Hydroponics*, Kangaroo Press, Australia, 1990
Mason J., *Growing Herbs*, Kangaroo Press, Australia, 1993

Trade Publications
International Plant Propagators Society (IPPS) Combined Proceedings
This is a collection of papers presented at several conferences held throughout the world, bound and published annually. The IPPS can be contacted at the following addresses:
Centre for Urban Horticulture, University of Washington, GF-15, Seattle, Washington, 98195, USA
Mrs K. Frances Biggs, PO Box 124, North Richmond, NSW, 2754, Australia Ph: (045) 71 1321
Mrs Janette Gaggini, Mears Ashby Nurseries Ltd, Glebe House, Glebe Rd, Mears Ashby, Northampton, NN6 ODL UK Ph: 0604) 811811

Australian Horticulture and HortiGuide, Rural Press, PO Box 1386, Collingwood, VIC 3066 Australia Ph: (03) 287 0900
Australian Nurseryman, PO Box 282, Parramatta, NSW 2150 Australia Ph: (02) 622 3199
Greenworld, Glenvale Publications, PO Box 376, Glen Waverley, VIC 3150 Australia Ph: (03) 544 2233
Successful Horticulture, Stirling Media, PO Box 670, Seven Hills, NSW 2147 Australia Ph: (02) 838 8233
American Nurseryman, 111 N. Canal St, Suite 545, Chicago, Illinios 60606, USA
Nursery Business, Brantwood Publications Inc., Northwood Plaza Station, Clearwater, Florida 33519-03060, USA

International Herb Growers and Marketers Association (Newsletters), PO Box 281, Silver Spring, Pennsylvania 17575, USA
The Grower Magazine, 50 Doughty St, London WC1N 2BR, England
Parks & Grounds (South Africa), Avonworld Publishing Co. P/L., PO Box 52068, Saxonworld 2132, South Africa

Other Books
Ball, G. Inc. *Ball Red Book*, Greenhouse Growing, Reston Publishing Co., Virginia, USA, 1985
Berninger, L. *Profitable Garden Centre Management*, Reston Publishing, USA, 1978
Browse P. *The Commercial Production of Climbing Plants*, Grower Books, UK, 1981
Davidson *et al. Nursery Management: Administration and Culture*, Prentice Hall, USA, 1988
Handreck, K. and Black, N. *Growing Media For Ornamental Plants and Turf*, New South Wales University Press, Sydney, 1984
Hartmann, H.T. Flocker, W.J. and Kofranek, A.M. *Plant Science: Growth, Development and Utilization of Cultivated Plants*, Prentice-Hall, USA, 1981
Hartmann, H. *et al. Plant Propagation: Principles and Practices*, Prentice Hall, USA, 1990
Horst, R.K. *Westcott's Plant Disease Handbook*, Van Nostrand Reinhold, USA, 1979
Joiner, J. *Foliage Plant Production*, Prentice Hall, USA, 1981
Kelly and Bowbrick. *Nursery Stock Manual*, Grower Books, UK, 1985
Macdonald, B. *Practical Woody Plant Propagation for Nursery Growers*, Timber Press, 1986
Nelson, P. *Greenhouse Operation and Management*, Prentice Hall, USA, 1991
Sullivan, G., Robertson J., and Staby, G. *Management For Retail Florists: With Applications To Nurseries And Garden Centers*, W.H. Freeman & Co., New York, 1980

Trends in the Retail Nursery Industry

1991 National Consumer and Retailer Study of Nursery Industry Opportunities
The following information is based on the National Consumer and Retailer Study of Nursery Industry Opportunities, published in the *Australian Nursery Magazine*, Vol 15. No 2, March 1991. The study was funded by the Australian nursery industry, through its statutory levy, the Horticultural Research and Development Corporation (HRDC) and the Australian Horticultural Corporation (AHC).

Consumer survey

In 1990 a total of 1407 residents participated in the national consumer survey. Some of the findings are included below:

Types of specialised gardens:
28% native bush garden
19% vegetable garden
12% cottage garden
125 rockery garden
11% rose garden
8% herb garden
4% rainforest garden
3% cactus garden
8% other

Major influences when choosing plants or garden accessories:
35% TV garden program
31% spouse
30% newspaper/magazine
26% friends/relatives
20% no one
15% nursery staff
9% radio gardening program

Awareness of retail nursery advertising and promotion:
44% any advertising remembered
31% letter box catalogues
25% garden shows
21% nursery front entrance displays
10% in store displays

Consumer needs from nurseries:
52% knowledgeable staff
46% good service
38% variety of products
38% helpful staff
36% friendly staff
34% easy parking
28% common plant names
27% good signage
25% good plant presentation
23% personal attention
18% guaranteed return
17% industry recognition
12% free delivery
6% playgrounds
5% self service
3% refreshments

Nursery retailers' survey

In 1990 a total of 202 nursery retailers were surveyed nationally. Some of the findings are included below:

Perception on demand increase or decrease:
Organic fertilisers and sprays 78% increasing sales, 5% decreasing sales, 17% static sales
Bedding plants 70% increasing sales, 9% decreasing sales, 21% static sales
Potted colour 67% increasing sales, 9% decreasing sales, 25% static sales
Herbs 61% increasing sales, 8% decreasing sales, 31% static sales
Perennials 58% increasing sales, 10% decreasing sales, 32% static sales
Trees/shrubs 52% increasing sales, 9% decreasing sales, 39% static sales
Citrus trees 50% increasing sales, 6% decreasing sales, 44% static sales

Satisfaction with plant or product quality supplied by wholesalers:
59% satisfied
15% neither
25% dissatisfied
(Sydney 33% and Adelaide 33% had highest proportion of dissatisfied retailers, Melbourne had least 16%.)

1991 Survey by Australian Horticultural Correspondence School

In 1991 the school surveyed its students on a national basis with the following results:

People were given a selection of different types of plants and asked which they grow in their own gardens. Response was as follows:

Vegetables	83%	Bonsai	5%
Natives	80%	Water Plants	12.5%
Orchids	23%	Indoor Plants	82%
Perennials	59%	Herbs	66%
Fruit Trees	80%	Azaleas	48%
Annual Flowers	71%	Lawn	66%

Contacts

Associations and Societies

The following list is by no means comprehensive, but it will provide points of contact in different parts of the world which will then lead you to other organisations.

International Plant Propagators Society
Centre for Urban Horticulture, University of Washington, GF-15, Seattle, Washington 98195, USA
Mrs K. Frances Biggs, PO Box 124, North Richmond, NSW 2754, Australia Ph: (045) 71 1321
Mrs Janette Gaggini, Mears Ashby Nurseries Ltd, Glebe House, Glebe Rd, Mears Ashby, Northampton, NN6 0DL, UK Ph: 0604 811811

Australian Nursery Industry Association
PO Box 282, Parramatta, NSW 2150 Australia Ph: (02) 622 3199

Australian Institute of Horticulture
PO Box 211, Strathfield, NSW 2137, Australia Ph: (02) 969 7128

British Institute of Horticulture
PO Box 313, 80 Vincent Sq., Westminster, London SW1P 2PE, UK

Garden Centre Association (UK)
30 Carey St, Reading, Berkshire RG1 7JS, UK

Royal Horticultural Society (UK)
80 Vincent Square, London SW1P 2PE, UK

American Association of Nurserymen
1250 1 Street, NW Suite 500, Washington, DC, 20005, USA

Equipment and Material Suppliers

Suppliers of equipment and materials can usually be found in the telephone directory or in trade directories or journals. Some suppliers are listed in these appendices. You may find that certain supplies are scarce in your locality and may need to be bought interstate or overseas. Seed supplies are one such example, and a range of selected seed suppliers are thus listed below. A more comprehensive list of Australian seed suppliers is available through the Australian Correspondence Schools (see address page 132).

Australian Seed Merchants

Bushland Flora
PO Box 312, Mt Evelyn, VIC 3796 Ph: (03) 736 4364, Fax: (03) 736 4716. Australian native grass and wetland species.

Bushland Flora
17 Trotman Cres, Yanchep, WA 6035 Ph: (09) 561 1636. West Australian native seeds.

Diggers Seeds
105 Latrobe Parade, Dromana, VIC 3936 Ph: (059) 87 1519. Wide range of vegetable, flower and perennial seeds.

D. Orriell — Seed Exporters
45 Frape Ave, Mt Yokine, WA 6060 Ph: (09) 344 2290, Fax: (09) 344 8982. Complete range of native and exotic seeds, including palms, cycads, everlastings, Proteaceae (Australian and South African). Lists available.

Eden Seeds
M.S. 316 Gympie, QLD 4570. Non-hybrid flower, perennial and shrub seeds.

Ellison Horticultural
PO Box 365, Nowra, NSW 2541 Ph: (044) 21 4255, Fax: (044) 23 0859. Extensive range of tree, shrub and palm seeds.

Erica Vale Seeds
PO Box 50, Jannali, NSW 2226 Ph: (02) 533 3593. Wide range of seeds, in particular flower and vegetable seeds.

Goodmans Seeds
PO Box 91, Bairnsdale, VIC 3875 Ph: (051) 52 4060, Fax: (051) 52 1671. Wide variety of flower and vegetable seeds.

Harper Seed Co.
Ranford St, Albany, WA 6330 Ph: (098) 41 7631

Henderson Seed Co.
PO Box 118, Bulleen, VIC 3105 Ph: (03) 850 2266, Fax: (03) 850 2266

Heritage Seeds
18 Industry Place, Bayswater, VIC 3153 Ph: (03) 720 5477. Pasture and lawn seed.

HG Kershaw Seeds
325 McCarrs Creek Rd, Terrey Hills, NSW 2084 Ph: (02) 450 2444. Wide range of native and exotic trees, shrubs and flowers.

Jerd Seeds
140 Madden Ave, Mildura, VIC 3500 Ph: Free call (008) 803 383; also 1 Orchid Crt, Park Orchids, VIC 3114 Ph: (03) 876 1525

Jodi Seeds
PO Box 288, Cleveland, QLD 4163. Australian natives.

Kings Herb Seeds
PO Box 975, Penrith, NSW 2751. Wide variety of herb, vegetable and flower varieties.

K-Palms Nursery
Poinciana Drive, Browns Plains, QLD 4118 Ph: (07) 800 1862

Landcare Services
Upper Beverley Rd, York, WA 6302. Ph: (096) 41 4064, Fax: (096) 41 4013. Native tree, shrub and wildflower seed for nurseries, landcare groups and large-scale rehabilitation.

M.L. Farrar P/l (International Seed Merchants)
PO Box 1046, Bomaderry, NSW 2541 Ph: (044) 21 7966, Fax: (044) 21 0051. Australian natives and exotics, palms, pasture seed (temperate to tropical).

New Gippsland Seed Farm
Queens Rd, Silvan, VIC 3795 Ph: (03) 737 9560. Vegetable seed suppliers.

Nindethana Seed Service
RMB 939, Woogenilup, WA 6324 Ph: (098) 54 1006, Fax: (098) 54 1011.

Largest selection of native seed in Australia, with more than 2500 species including many rare and unusual lines. Suppliers of bulk seeds for rehabilitation work. Send SAE for free catalogue.

Northrup King Seeds
PO Box 335, Dandenong, VIC 3175 Ph: (03) 706 3033, Fax: (03) 706 3182. Wide range, including flowers, vegetables and perennials.

Pacific Seeds
Kunnanurra, WA 6743 Ph: (091) 68 1172

Phoenix Seeds
Channel Hwy, Snug, TAS 7054 Ph: (002) 67 9663

Q-Hort
PO Box 595, Cleveland, QLD 4163 Ph: (07) 821 0745, Fax: (07) 821 0746

Specialty Seeds
Hawthorn Park, Chanters Lane, Tylden, VIC 3444

Tropigro P L
Lot 1554 Farrell Crescent, Winnellie, NT 0820 Ph: (089) 84 3200

Vaughans Wildflower Seeds
C/- PO Gingin, WA 6503 Ph: (095) 75 7551. Wide range of Australian native species, in particular West Australian. Catalogue available on request.

Walz Seeds Australia
PO Box 5579, Gold Coast Mail Centre, QLD 4127 Ph: (075) 37 9133

West Australian Wildflower Seed Co.
11 Bertram Rd, Darlington, WA 6070 Ph: (09) 299 6280. Wide variety of West Australian natives in packages or larger amounts.

International Seed Merchants

Bejo
PO Box 50, Warmenhuizen, Holland

Booker Seeds Ltd
Boston Rd, Sleaford, Lincolnshire, NG34 7HA, UK

Breeders Seeds
17 Summerwood La. Halsall, Ormskirk, Lancs, L39 8RQ, UK

CN Seeds
Denmark House, Pymoor, Ely, Cambs, CB6 2EG, UK

Colegrave Seeds Ltd
Milton Rd, West Adderbury, Banbury, Oxon, OX17 3EY, UK

Kings Herb Seeds (New Zealand)
PO Box 19-084, Avondale, Auckland, New Zealand Ph: (09) 887 588, Fax: (09) 828 7588. Wide variety of herb, vegetable and flower seeds.

Nickerson Seed Specialist Ltd
JNRC, Rothwell, Lincoln, LN7 DT

Nova Tree Enterprises
RR2, Middle Musquodoboit, Nova Scotia, Canada, BON 1XO

Royal Sluis Ltd
PO Box 34, Leyland, Preston, PR5 3QT, UK

Samuel Yates Ltd
Withyfold Dve, Macclesfield, Cheshire, SK10 2BE, UK

Silverhill Seeds
18 Silverhill Crescent, Kenilworth, 7700, South Africa Ph: (21) 762 4245, Fax: (21) 797 6609. Specialist in South African natives. Proteaceae, Ericaceae, Geraniaceae, bulbs, succulents, annuals, perennials, trees and shrubs. Catalogue available.

Walters Seed & Nursery
4645 62nd Street, Holland, Michigan, 49423, USA

Glossary

Bare-rooted plants   These are plants that have been 'lifted' from their growing area without the soil or growing media left around their roots. This is common for many deciduous ornamental trees (e.g. elms, ashes, maples) and fruit trees (e.g. apricot, apple, peach, pear), and shrubs such as roses. The plants should be planted as soon as possible to prevent the roots drying out. They can be temporarily stored if the roots are covered with a moist material such as peat moss, straw, or rotted sawdust.

Bedding plants   These are plants used for temporary displays, generally planted out in warmer seasons (e.g. many annuals).

Bottom heat   This is where heat is applied at, or near, the base of plants to stimulate growth. This can be done in a variety of ways, including under bench heating with heat cables or hot water pipes, heating of floors in greenhouses using heat cables, or composting materials such as sawdust or manures. (See also Hotbed).

Coldframe   This is in effect a mini-greenhouse. Generally unheated, they are commonly used to provide protection for plants being propagated, or for plants that may need a short period of protection against extremes of climate. They have the advantage of being readily moveable, and easy to construct.

Dibble stick   This is a short pencil-like stick that is used to make holes in growing media for the potting-up ('pricking out') of seedlings, or for inserting or potting up cuttings.

Flats   These are shallow trays with drainage holes in the bottom, which are commonly for germinating seeds or rooting cuttings.

Forcing   The use of heat and altered light conditions to induce very early flowering, or very tall growth. Commonly used in cut flower production.

Growing media   Any material in which plants are being grown can be classified as a growing media. This includes soil, soilless potting mixes, rockwool, vermiculite, even water (i.e. hydroponics).

Hotbed   This is a bed used for plant propagation that provides heat to the base of seed trays or to pots of cuttings to stimulate germination in seedlings and subsequent root growth, and root initiation and growth in cuttings. Heat is normally supplied from either hot water pipes, or from resistance cables which, when an electric current is passed through them, heats up. These heating elements generally have some material such as propagating sand, vermiculite, gravel or perlite placed around them to help spread (diffuse) the heat.

Juvenility   A stage of a plant's life following the germination of a seed to produce a seedling. Vegetative growth dominates, and juvenile plants cannot respond to flower-inducing stimuli. In some plants juvenile foliage differs markedly from adult foliage (e.g. some eucalypts). In difficult-to-root plants, taking cutting material from stock plants in a juvenile phase will often give better results than using older (adult growth phase) material.

Living colour Plants cultivated to provide colourful displays (i.e.displays of foliage, flowers, fruit). These can be either grown in-ground or in containers, and be grown for either short or long term display.

Micropropagation This is the production (propagation) of plants from very small plant parts, tissues or cells. They are grown under aseptic (sterile) conditions in a highly controlled environment. The term tissue culture is a collective term used to describe a number of in-vitro procedures used in culturing plant tissue, including producing haploid plant cells and artificial hybridisation.

Plugs These are individual plants, or small clumps of plants, that are grown in trays containing large numbers of individual cells. For example, the tray may have 18 cells across by 32 cells along, making a total 576 cells per tray, with each individual cell having measuring 20 x 20 mm and with a depth of 30 mm. Each cell has an individual drainage hole. The trays are filled with a growing medium and seed is planted into each cell, either by hand (very slow) or by machine. There are machines that are capable of planting individual seeds into each cell, and very quickly. The trays are made of plastic, that has some degree of flexibility so that it can be bent a little to allow easy removal of individual plugs (root ball and growing media combined). This type of growing system, is ideal for flower and vegetable seedlings, and can be highly mechanised (e.g. filling trays with soil, seeding, potting up individual plugs).

Potted colour Plants grown in containers to provide a colourful display. They are commonly used as an alternative to cut flowers (e.g. Chyrsanthemums in 150 mm pots), and are generally discarded once their peak display (e.g. flowering) has finished.

Provenance This is also known as 'seed origin' and refers to where the seed has been produced. This can give an indication of the particular genetic characteristics of the seed (e.g. size, shape, flower colour, adaptation to climatic conditions, resistance to pest and diseases, tolerance to different soil conditions).

Scarification This is any process that breaks, scratches, cuts, mechanically alters, or softens seed coats to make them more impermeable to water and gases. Techniques include dipping in hot water, dipping in concentrated sulphuric acid, removing hard seed coats with sandpaper, and nicking seed coats with a sharp knife.

Standards These are where plants are grown as a single tall stem (e.g. some fruit trees and roses). Some prostrate cultivars are also budded or grafted onto taller stemmed rootstocks to create pendulous forms (e.g. weeping elm, *Grevillea gaudi-chaudi* and *Grevillea* Royal Mantle).

Stock plants These are the parent plants from which cutting propagation material is obtained. There are three main sources of stock plant material. These are i) plants growing in parks, around houses, in the wild, etc. ii) prunings or trimmings from young nursery plants, and iii) plants grown specifically as a source of cutting material. Stock plants should be correctly identified (and true to type), and in a healthy condition.

Stratification This is where dormant seeds that have imbibed water are subjected to a period of chilling to 'after-ripen' the embryo. This process is also known as moist-chilling. Dry seeds should be soaked in water prior to stratification. Seeds are then usually mixed with some sort of moisture retaining material, such as coarse washed sand, or peat or sphagnum moss, or vermiculite. The material should be moistioned prior to mixing. The mix is then stored at a temperature of 0–10°C. The lower shelf of a domestic refrigerator is usually suitable. The time of stratification will depend on seed type, but usually is 1–4 months. In areas with cool winters, stratification can be carried out in beds outdoors, but seeds should be protected from pests such as birds or mice.

Tissue culture *see* Micropropagation

Tubes Small, narrow containers, commonly used for the first potting-up stage of newly propagated seed or cuttings. The tube-like nature encourages new roots to grow straight down, reducing the risk of roots coiling. A common 'tube' used in Australia has an upper diameter of 50 mm, a depth of around 70 mm, tapering down to a lower diameter of about 40 mm. This type is most widely used in producing stock for planting up into larger containers. Deeper tubes are also commonly used for tubing-up fast-growing seedlings that are to be used in large-scale plantings (e.g. reafforestation, farms, trees). Some nurseries specialise in tubestock production for sale to retail and growing-on nurseries.

Tubestock   Plants grown in tube-like containers (see Tubes above).

Wounding   Root production on cuttings can often be promoted by wounding the base of cuttings. A common method of wounding plants is to cut away a thin strip of bark, about 1.5 to 3 cm long (this will depend on the size of the cutting) from each side of the cutting near the base. The strip should not be cut too deeply, just enough to expose the cambium layer (the soft layer of new growth between the wood and the bark), without cutting very deeply into the wood beneath.

Index